Bernard Denvir
is the author of a four-volume documentary history
of taste in art, architecture and design in Britain,
as well as of books on Chardin, Post-Impressionism, Fauvism
and of *Impressionism: The Painters and the Paintings* (1991).
A contributor to many journals and magazines, he was head of
the Department of Art History at Ravensbourne College of Art and Design,
a member of the Council for National Academic Awards,
and for several years President of the British section
of the International Association of Art Critics.
His other books include *The Impressionists at First Hand* (1987),
The Encyclopaedia of Impressionism (1989) and *Toulouse-Lautrec* (1991),
also in the World of Art series.

WORLD OF ART

This famous series
provides the widest available
range of illustrated books on art in all its aspects.
If you would like to receive a complete list
of titles in print please write to:

THAMES AND HUDSON
30 Bloomsbury Street, London WC1B 3QP
In the United States please write to:
THAMES AND HUDSON INC.
500 Fifth Avenue, New York, New York 10110

BERNARD DENVIR

Post-Impressionism

148 illustrations, 24 in color

Thames and Hudson

*First published in the United States in 1992 by
Thames and Hudson Inc., 500 Fifth Avenue,
New York, New York 10110*

Library of Congress Catalog Card Number 91–65995

Printed and bound in Singapore

Contents

GAZERS AT PAINTINGS FEW APPRECIATE AND FEWER UNDERSTAND: STUDIES AT THE GRAFTON GALLERIES.

1 'Post-Impressionist Expressions', *Illustrated London News* 3 December 1910

Introduction

The term 'Post-Impressionism' first made its appearance in the summer of 1910 in the course of a discussion between two English critics, Roger Fry and Desmond MacCarthy, about an exhibition of French paintings they were organizing to take place later in the year at the Grafton Galleries off Bond Street. MacCarthy recorded the event thirty-five years later in *The Listener*:

Roger and I and a young journalist who was helping us with publicity met to consider this [i.e. a title for the exhibition]. Roger first suggested various terms such as 'Expressionism', which aimed at distinguishing these artists from the Impressionists, but the journalist wouldn't have that or any of his alternatives. At last Roger, losing patience, said 'Oh, let's just call them Post-Impressionists. At any rate, they came after the Impressionists.'

The works in the exhibition, which eventually opened on 5 November to howls of execration from the press, included over 30 by Gauguin, 20 by van Gogh, 21 by Cézanne, 8 oils and a pastel by Manet and smaller numbers of representative works by Seurat, Signac, Cross, Denis, Sérusier, Vallotton, Vlaminck and Picasso. It was what can only be described as a traumatic success, engendering a vast amount of publicity, emphasizing the emergence of 'modern' art, but polarizing opinions and attitudes about art into a state of confrontation which was to persist throughout most of the century. Virginia Woolf's statement that 'on or about December 1910 human nature changed' was not quite such a hyperbole as it might seem.

Sixty-nine years after the Grafton Galleries' exhibition, another one devoted to Post-Impressionism was held in the Royal Academy, London. It contained 428 paintings drawn from nine countries. Some idea of how far the stylistic formula invented by Fry had become extended may be derived from the fact that in the French section, in addition to works by those generally accepted as Post-Impressionists, were paintings by main line Impressionists such as Renoir, Monet and Degas, by society portraitists such as Besnard and Tissot and by genre painters such as Paul Legrand and Jean Béraud.

The problem of the meaning of Post-Impressionism is compounded by the fact that Fry's contribution to the categorization of art history has never won universal acceptance; it is largely confined to the English-speaking world – mainly Britain. Moreover, many of the styles and movements discernible within the implications of Post-Impressionism, Symbolism for instance, though they may have had their origin in France, produced some of their most impressive manifestations outside that country. To attempt to cover so manifest a diversity as that implied by the 1979 Royal Academy exhibition would be impossible in a work of this scope, and in any case would be to enlarge the concept of Post-Impressionism – in reality virtually all developments in art that followed Impressionism, up to Cubism – to

such a degree as seriously to diminish its value as a meaningful art historical concept. In a book of this kind one is also tempted to avoid devoting too much space to artists such as Cézanne and van Gogh whose importance and influence are enormous but who are, in a sense, too 'great' and their work too complex to be confined within the category of Post-Impressionism, and to concentrate rather on less well-known figures who are more representative. I have therefore confined the scope primarily to an examination of those French artists who, in the twenty years or so following the final Impressionist exhibition in 1886, sought to find an alternative artistic orthodoxy in differing techniques and ideologies, and of the varying contexts in which they did so.

2 Roger Fry *A Room at the 2nd Post-Impressionist Exhibition* 1912

3 Seurat *Model seated in Profile* 1887

CHAPTER ONE

A Divided Legacy

The eighth, and last, Impressionist exhibition, described merely as
'Eighth Exhibition' – the word independent had been dropped
because of the recent foundation of the Groupe des Indépendants (*see*
p. 39) – opened on 15 May 1886 on the second floor of a prestigious
café, the Maison Dorée on the corner of the rue Lafitte and the
boulevard des Italiens. It had been a close run thing and it quickly
became evident why the word 'Impressionist' had not been used in the
publicity. Only three of the participating artists, Berthe Morisot,
Armand Guillaumin and Gauguin, showed works which could   8
strictly be called Impressionist, while Mary Cassatt and Degas showed
a number of pastels, those of the latter being entitled 'Series of nudes
of women bathing, drying, rubbing down, combing their hair, or   12
having it combed'. Although the situation had been complicated by
the fact that the dealer Paul Durand-Ruel was assembling three
hundred Impressionist paintings to take to America, the main reason
for the absence of some of the major figures of the movement sprang
from internal dissensions. The Impressionists had never been the
happy band of brothers they have been made out to be. Even in the
early days at the Café Guerbois, Manet and Degas had shared a
profound antipathy to each other, competing in behind-the-back
jibes which ranged from aspersions about sexual appetite to
accusations of artistic incompetence. Renoir couldn't stand Pissarro,
to whom he always referred as 'that Israelite'; Caillebotte saw Degas
as a scheming Macchiavelli and Degas himself was intermittently
bitchy about almost everybody Mary Cassatt excluded, but that was
at least partly because, as one of the main financial supporters of the
group, she was approved by all.

Underlying these animosities, which are not unusual in any
professional group, there was a basic dichotomy, which echoed the
earlier duality of Ingres and Delacroix, between line and colour,
between thought and feeling, between form and atmosphere. This
had been apparent at the 1881 exhibition, with Degas, that archetypal
classicist, Mary Cassatt, Raffaëlli, Rouault and Zandomeneghi on   4

one side and Monet, Renoir, Pissarro, Sisley and Gauguin on the other. The position was further complicated by a dissension between those such as Renoir, Monet, Manet and Cézanne who were more than happy to exhibit at the Salon and those who were not.

Before this particular exhibition opened, Caillebotte had written to Pissarro expressing a disquiet shared by many:

What is to become of our exhibitions? This is my well-considered opinion; we ought to continue, and continue only in an artistic direction, the only direction in the long run that is of interest to us all. I suggest therefore that a show should be composed of all those who have contributed anything of real interest to the movement, that is you, Monet, Renoir, Sisley, Mme. Morisot, Mlle. Cassatt, Cézanne, Guillaumin, if you wish Gauguin, perhaps Cordey and myself. That's all, since Degas refuses a show on such a basis. I should like to know how passionately interested the general public is in our personal squabbles. It's very naive of us to quarrel about such things. It was Degas who introduced disunity in our midst. He spends all his time arguing at the Nouvelle-Athènes or in parties. He would do better to paint a little more . . . No, this man has gone sour. He doesn't hold such an important place as he thinks his talents deserve, and though he will never admit it, bears the whole world a grudge.

4 Zandomeneghi *Place d'Anvers, Paris* 1880

5 Seurat *Une Baignade à Asnières* 1883–4

By 1886 all the rancour and all the opposing ideas of the very nature of Impressionism had become polarized through the emergence of a new figure with startlingly new technical ideas – and the movement itself had primarily been a technical revolution. Ever since he was 16 – or so he said – Georges Seurat had been preoccupied with the quest for 'a formula for optical painting' and, an early devotee of Impressionism, had read the works of Eugène Chevreul, the scientist who had written about the depiction and apprehension of colour. Seurat's first important works were conté crayon drawings, careful exercises in the balancing of light and shade with a concern for the expression of plastic values – he was an admirer of Ingres. Round about 1882 he started working in small panels painted in small strokes and showing an extraordinary chromatic brilliance. In the following year he produced his first major work, *Une Baignade à Asnières*, in which he exploited for the first time in a 'scientific' and 'objective' way a method based on the writings of Ogden N. Rood, David Sutter, Chevreul and others – the notion of juxtaposing colours so as to be combined in the spectator's eye, thereby obtaining the vibratory quality of light as seen in nature. Although the Impressionists had sometimes used a similar method, it was on an instinctive rather than a dogmatic basis. At the same time too, though in *Une Baignade* Seurat had chosen a subject, ordinary people disporting themselves on the banks of the Seine, which would have appealed to Monet, Renoir or Sisley, his pictorial approach was very different from theirs. It was a monumental work (2 by 2.9 metres), monumentally composed, and was the outcome of numerous preliminary studies, a work far removed from the instantaneous, *plein air* approach of the Impressionists (though it should be noted that Seurat too did his preliminary sketches in the open air).

Here was a way of painting which removed from the artist the onerous burden of spontaneity, which provided him with a secure framework within which to work and wherein, without the need of daily inspiration, he could work contentedly away according to a preordained plan. In fact, of course, things weren't as simple as all that. Pointillism, Divisionism or Neo-Impressionism, as it came to be variously called, was no system of, as it were, painting by numbers, but it was very seductive to those who were discontented by what they saw as the hit or miss approach of Impressionism. *Une Baignade* was exhibited – badly hung in a canteen – at the first Indépendants exhibition of 1884. There it was seen by the 21-year-old Paul Signac, who had virtually taught himself painting, as he explained in a letter to Monet in 1880:

I have been painting for two years, and my only models have been your own works. I have been following the wonderful path you opened up to us. I have always worked regularly and conscientiously, but without any advice or help, for I do not know any Impressionist painter who would be able to guide me.

Monet seems to have declined this touching proposal but the persuasive young man got into contact with Guillaumin and sedulously followed his mentor in painting pictures of the industrial banks of the Seine in Paris. He was greatly impressed by the work of Seurat, whose theories he was to define and expand and whose mantle as the leader of Pointillism he was to assume on the latter's death at the age of 32 in 1891. They were joined by Henri Edmond Cross – his real name was Delacroix but his art school teacher had advised him to take another to avoid attracting comparisons with his famous homonym – whose work till this time had been in the tradition of academic realism. How unmechanical the style they had adopted really was can be gauged by

14

6 Signac *The Dining-room: Breakfast* 1886–7

7 Signac *Les femmes au puit* 1892

the difference between their works. Seurat, incomparably the greatest of the three, was a vital, exuberant painter with a sense of pictorial magnificence. Signac was more reserved and careful in his approach, whilst Cross was much more emotional, a painter of colour rather than of light, sometimes close to Monet, sometimes suggesting the advent of the Fauves – indeed he was to have a considerable influence on the young Matisse early in the next century.

10, 14

The fourth immediate convert to the theories of Seurat and Signac, whom he had met through their mutual friend Guillaumin, was Pissarro. There could have been few more convincing demonstrations of the dilemmas of Impressionism and the reactions of those who were its immediate successors than this startling conversion. One of the founding fathers of Impressionism and for some twenty years one of its most consistent practitioners, Pissarro had always tended to be nervously eclectic, anxious to weigh the varying advantages of his contemporaries' works and driven by his own relative failure to obtain quite the same reputation or quite the same prices that Renoir and Monet were already achieving, profoundly insecure. Deeply introspective and given to prolific letter writing, he had a passion for ideologies and his constant attempts to find in his political convictions a dynamism for his art suggests how vulnerable he would have been to the assured, anxiety-free dogmas of his young friends. He started to paint in their manner, with some refinements of his own, towards the end of 1885, being especially satisfied with the contrast it made with the 'rough' style of main-line Impressionism.

9

8 Guillaumin *Le Pont de Marie* 1883

9 Pissarro *Femme dans un clos, soleil de printemps dans le pré* 1887

10 Cross *The Excursionists* 1894

16

11 Seurat *La Grande Jatte* 1883–6

12 Degas *Woman drying Herself* 1885

Seurat in the meantime was working on another great compo-
11 sition, *A Sunday Afternoon on the Island of the Grande Jatte* (*La Grande
Jatte*), in which, heartened by enthusiasm shown by Pissarro, he
constructed the whole paint surface with tiny round dots or points,
instead of small brush-strokes. It was this work which – along with
some drawings and landscapes as well as works by Signac – was to
precipitate the symbolic end of Impressionism as a coherent
movement. The preparation of the 1886 exhibition was in the hands
of Berthe Morisot and her husband, Manet's brother Eugène. Early in
March Pissarro wrote to his son Lucien:

I had a violent set-to with M. Eugène Manet about Seurat and Signac. The
latter was present and so was Guillaumin. I soundly berated M. Manet,
which, as you can imagine, did not please Renoir. Anyway, the point is this, I
explained to Manet, who doesn't seem to have understood anything I said,
that Seurat had something new to contribute, which these gentlemen

probably didn't understand despite their talent, that I am personally
convinced of the progressive character of his art, and certain that in time it
will yield extraordinary results. I do not accept the snobbish judgments of
'romantic Impressionists' to whose interests it is to resist new tendencies. In
brief, I accept the challenge. But before anything is done they want to stack
the cards, and ruin the exhibition. M. Manet was beside himself, but I didn't
give in . . . I told Degas that Seurat's painting was very interesting. 'I would
have noted that myself, Pissarro, were it not that the thing is so big.' Very
well, if Degas sees nothing in it, so much the worse for him. This simply
means that there's something precious which he can't understand. We shall
see. M. Manet would have liked to prevent Seurat from showing his figure
paintings (*La Grande Jatte*). I protested against this, telling Manet that if that
were the case, we would make no concessions, and that if space were lacking
we would restrict the number of our own exhibits, but that we would fight
anybody who would impose his choice on us. Still I suppose things will sort
themselves out somehow.

13 Seurat *The Bathers*, *c.* 1883, study for *Une Baignade*

14 Cross *L'Air du Soir* 1893–4

In the event they did. Seurat, Signac, Pissarro, his son Lucien and all the Pointillists or Neo-Impressionists except Cross were quarantined in a room of their own. Gauguin, who had been participating in the exhibitions since 1879, was accepted but so, to the annoyance of Pissarro and others, was his friend the amiable ex-banker Émile Schuffenecker, whose paintings were generally accepted as being a good deal less than mediocre but whose devotion to Gauguin was virtually boundless. He was not unique in his artistic mediocrity and many of the exhibitors fell even below his standards. A newcomer was Odilon Redon, who sent in a selection of drawings.

Monet did not exhibit, partly because he didn't approve of Gauguin and Schuffenecker, partly because he wanted to exhibit at Georges Petit's 'Exposition Internationale', which he rightly saw as being potentially more remunerative. Renoir felt the same and both

Sisley and Caillebotte thought that the exhibition as a whole was a betrayal of the basic principles of Impressionism. Criticism amongst the press was not so much hostile as muted and was complicated by the fact that several critics got Signac and Seurat confused – just as earlier they had confused Monet and Manet. George Moore had to go down on his knees signature hunting before he could differentiate between the works of Seurat and those of Pissarro. But the exhibition did provoke from 25-year-old Félix Fénéon a review which in its sense of historical perspective and acuteness of understanding provided an apologia for the works of Seurat, Signac and Pissarro and, by placing them in their correct relationship to Impressionism, implicitly mapped out a programme for the successors of 'the heroic age of Impressionism'. He divided his article into three sections, each represented by a major figure – Degas, Gauguin and Seurat. Degas he saw as standing for a more realistic concept of life than that of the major Impressionists, his pastels portraying 'dim furnished rooms and wretched hovels in which these bodies with their richly textured skin, bodies bruised and moulded by whoring, child-bearing and illness, scrub and stretch out their limbs'. Gauguin he saw not so much as an Impressionist as someone who was more concerned with expressing emotion and feelings than with recording, however exquisitely, natural phenomena. 'The muffled harmony in M. Paul Gauguin's paintings flows from the close-set tones he uses. Dense trees gush from rich, humid, lush soil, overflowing the frame, banishing the sky. A heavy air. A glimpse of bricks suggests a nearby house, hides stretch, muzzles part the brushwood – cows.' Finally Fénéon, after reviewing the history of Impressionism, hailed Seurat and his followers as the precursors of a new scientific art, free from the arbitrary techniques of Impressionism, which used 'tenebrous sauces concocted on the palette' and relied on happy accidents – 'a brush dragged over a green landscape gave the impression of red'. In stating the scientific principles which underlay Seurat's work and analysing their effects (*see* pp. 139–42), Fénéon was showing himself to be one of the first critics adequately to explain an artist's technique and intentions and also converting *La Grande Jatte* into what Signac described as 'the manifesto painting' of a new movement.

A more serious blow, however, was also struck against the accepted verities of Impressionism from a totally unexpected quarter. Zola published his *L'Oeuvre* in 1886 which, like all his works, reached a huge audience and gave the impression that the man who had done so much to defend the movement was in his more mature years rejecting

15 Cézanne *Still Life with Onions and a Bottle* 1895–1900

it. The theme of the novel was the unsuccessful attempt of a young painter to produce a masterpiece that would realize his dreams and bring him fame. The character of this *héros maudit* was clearly based on Cézanne, with additional traits supplied by Manet, and the whole book based on the history of the Impressionists. Basically it repeated criticisms which Zola had levied against the Impressionists six years earlier and which were originally printed in a Russian periodical but maliciously reprinted in *Le Figaro* in 1880:

All the Impressionists are poor technicians. In the arts as well as in literature form alone sustains new ideas and new methods. All these artists are too easily contented. They woefully neglect the solidity of works meditated on for a long time and for this reason it is to be feared that they are merely preparing the path for the great artist of the future expected by the world.

Whatever Zola's intentions in the novel had been, the public saw it as an attack on the Impressionists.

The irony of it was that Cézanne, although his constant struggles to achieve his painterly goal coincided with those of Claude Lantier, the hero of the book, was the least Impressionist of all the Impressionists, and furiously concerned with the 'solidity' of his works. His constant concern was to make a 'new museum art' to re-do Poussin, an artist whose name never appeared on the lips of any Impressionist other than Degas. He was, in fact, the first Post-Impressionist to make, as did the Pointillists and eventually the Cubists, a structural analysis of nature, producing an art of the mind concerned with the emotional apprehension of formal qualities in mountains, women or onions and 15 totally unconcerned with the evanescent effects of light, shade and atmosphere that so exercised painters such as Monet, Sisley or Renoir. A self-imposed exile in his native Aix-en-Provence had largely isolated him from the Paris art world but in 1895 Ambroise Vollard organized an exhibition of 150 of his works shown in three successive sections. Warmly approved by his fellow Impressionists, Cézanne's work was a revelation to younger artists and the admiration it aroused in them was celebrated in a painting by Denis shown at the Salon of 1901 entitled *Homage to Cézanne*, which showed Vuillard, Bonnard, 16 Vollard, Redon, Denis himself and others gathered around a still life by the master. Amongst the considerable number of buyers at the exhibition was the 26-year-old Henri Matisse, who paid 1300 francs for the *Bathers* of *c.* 1880. It was to him – too shy to visit an artist whom he so ardently admired – that Cézanne's widow was later to confide, 'You know Cézanne didn't know what he was doing. He didn't know how to finish his pictures. Renoir and Monet both knew their craft as painters.'

16   The painting which the group in Denis's tribute was admiring was a still life once owned by Gauguin, who in the 1880s possessed six of Cézanne's works, at least one of which he copied and all of which played an important role in his own development, even though the older artist was at one point suspicious that this brash young man was intent on stealing what he called his sensations. Gauguin was incessant in his praise of Cézanne and retained for a long time the still life, which features in the background of a portrait of a Breton woman painted in Le Pouldu in 1890.

    Insofar as one important aspect of the reaction against Impressionism took the shape of a desire for structure, order and a classical
17 approach to painting, Cézanne was more influential than the Pointillists, spectacular and symbolic though their achievement was. Pissarro, finding the new style unpopular and yearning after the lyric certainties of his earlier work, confessed to Henry van de Velde, one of the organizers of the Brussels-based Les Vingt (XX) exhibitions (*see* p. 40) which had given a good deal of space to Seurat and his followers:

Having tried this theory for four years and having now abandoned it, not without painful and obstinate struggles to regain what I had lost, and not to

16 Denis *Homage to Cézanne* 1900

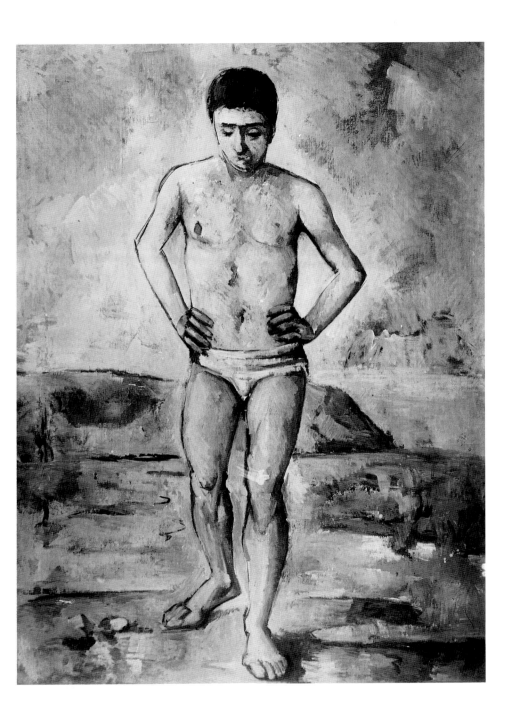

17 Cézanne *The Large Bather, c.* 1885

lose what I had learned, I can no longer consider myself one of the neo-Impressionists who abandon movement and life for a diametrically opposed aesthetic, which perhaps is the right thing for the man with the right temperament, but it is not right for me, anxious as I am to avoid all narrow, so-called scientific theories. Having found, after many attempts (I speak for myself) that it was impossible to be true to my sensations and consequently to render life and movement, impossible to be faithful to the so random and so admirable effects of nature, impossible to give an individual character to my drawing, I had to give up.

In the event he not only gave up but destroyed or repainted many of his Pointillist works, which in any case had been Pointillist in only the most superficial way.

Pissarro was not unique in his flirtation with the new art. Vincent van Gogh had moved to a Paris dominated by the Impressionists but he was slow to subscribe to any particular formula. His friendship with Pissarro led him to look with a kindly eye on Seurat and he became quite intimate with Signac, who persuaded him to use the new technique in a number of works such as those they painted when on expeditions together in and around the suburb of Asnières. Writing to his brother Théo about Seurat he noted, 'He is an original colourist, and Signac likewise, though to a different degree. The Pointillists have found something new, and I quite like them after all.' He realized, however, the temporal limitations of the style:

I think that it is a real discovery, yet it can already be foreseen that this technique will not become a universal dogma any more than any other. This
11 is another reason why Seurat's *Grande Jatte*, the landscapes in large dots by Signac and Anquetin's *Boat* will become in time still more individual and still more original.

Yet, although he did not remain a practising Pointillist, the technique in a modified form often showed through in his brushwork. His hatred of any kind of stylistic dogma made him fit uneasily into any of the accepted categories of Post-Impressionism, even though he was in a sense one of its greatest figures, linking colour with symbolism and feeling in a way which was followed by subsequent artists for the next
18 century. He himself, for instance, called *The Night Café* of 1888 'one of the ugliest things I have done' – because of the crudity of the colours, the clash of disparate greens and reds, the sulphurous-looking floor matched by the uncanny light from the lamps, all creating 'an atmosphere like that of a devil's furnace, of pale sulphur, like the powers of darkness in a tavern'. But he used the phrase proudly, not contritely, and later thought of the work as one of the most important

18 Van Gogh *The Night Café* 1888

he had done, comparing it with his earlier *Potato-eaters*. When he was considering making meticulous copies of his works this was one he specifically mentioned as having to be included in the project. Unconnected with Synthetism, Pointillism, Symbolism or any other of the groups which sought to replace Impressionism as new artistic orthodoxies, van Gogh's works were reflected in all of them as a vindication of the abstract use of colour in contradiction to its role as a means of achieving optical realism.

Gauguin, although he produced one or two paintings in a Pointillist style, was constitutionally averse to anything which smacked of scientific principle. Of much greater significance was his complex relationship with van Gogh and the light it throws on the

29

various allegiances and principles which struggled for dominance amongst a generation which was aware that Impressionism no longer satisfied its needs or expressed its intentions. In a letter written to Émile Bernard shortly after his arrival in Arles in 1888, Gauguin commented, 'Generally speaking Vincent and I hardly ever see eye to eye. He admires Daumier, Daubigny, Ziem and the great (Théodore) Rousseau, all people whom I cannot tolerate. On the other hand he hates Ingres, Raphael, Degas, all of whom I admire.' There could not have been a neater line up of the two divergent traditions which painting was to follow through the next few decades, the romantics of one sort lined up on one side, the classicists on the other. But the reality was far more complex. Gauguin was as romantic as anybody and, though van Gogh was constantly acknowledging his debt to

19 Gauguin *Night Café at Arles* 1888

20 Van Gogh *L'Arlésienne* 1888

him, he owed as much to the painter whom he was always treating as his pupil. Gauguin's use of liberated colour was influenced as much by van Gogh as by his own instincts, the major difference being that, unmoved by a passionate ecstasy of feeling, he substituted for it either a diffused sexuality or the more accessible resonances of a system of accepted symbols.

Accepting or rejecting either Impressionism or any one of its upcoming rivals was never simple. Toulouse-Lautrec was a case in point. He had been painting since childhood and when he was a student at the atelier of Cormon had come, like all young painters, under the influence of Impressionism, conceiving for Degas a respect which, as usual with that sharp-tongued man, was returned with something approaching contempt. It was to remain the dominant element in his painting style for most of his short life, modified, largely under the influence of Pissarro, by a system of loose brush-strokes applied in a criss-cross fashion, spontaneously and quickly. Although he knew and admired Seurat with whom he shared elements of iconography – circuses and café concerts – he was tempted not at all by the doctrinaire approach of Pointillism. Mainly through his friendship with the Natansons and his work for *La Revue Blanche* (*see* p. 165), Lautrec was in close contact with Vuillard, Bonnard and the other Nabis (*see* Chapter 4), who undoubtedly owed as much to his work as they did to a shared interest in Japanese prints. But the influence of Lautrec derived not from his paintings but from his graphic work with its free, bounding lines, its areas of flat colour, its decorative distortion, its use of rhythmic patterning and above all else from its popularization of the print. This was to be one of the most characteristic outlets of the whole Post-Impressionist period, allowing artists a freedom to innovate and explore. It not only influenced his immediate contemporaries but was to stretch forward to Matisse, Picasso and the artists of the first half of the twentieth century. Unexpectedly, Toulouse-Lautrec was more important in this respect than his fellow-student, the sharply ambitious Louis Anquetin who, having been influenced by Renoir, dabbled in Pointillism and evolved with Bernard the style they called 'Cloisonnism' (*see* p. 78).

42, 57 He started to paint pictures, mainly concerned with contemporary life, which translated directly into pastel, oil and canvas the kind of innovations that Lautrec and others had achieved in the graphic arts.

Innovation, of course, was not the only answer to the disquiets with Impressionism which the younger generation was feeling. The revelation of Cézanne had been of great significance; Degas was admired not only by Lautrec but also by Gauguin, Seurat and others; Monet's use of bold colours woven together by improvisatory brushwork was influential on van Gogh. Then there were those who, though contemporaries of the Impressionists, had never succumbed to their doctrines. Chief amongst them was Puvis de Chavannes, who was 62 when the last Impressionist exhibition opened, had studied under Delacroix and been formatively influenced by Chassériau. To a generation sated with the easy hedonism of the Impressionists, and sufficiently discontented with the squalid manifestations of greed and competitiveness which it saw as underpinning bourgeois society, his rather ostentatious nobility and idealism, his apparent quest for an art of classic order and ideal stability and his appeal to the 'higher' emotions were infinitely beguiling. The diametric opposite of Moreau, who was also experiencing a surge of popularity at this time, his poetic austerity, subdued colours and generalized harmony of composition presented what seemed a seductive alternative to the mundane. Téodor de Wyzéwa, editor of *La Revue Wagnérienne* and an art critic of repute, put the view of a whole generation when he wrote in 1894:

The work of Puvis de Chavannes represents for us a reaction against opposite excesses of which we have grown tired. In painting as well as in literature a moment came when we had enough, and indeed too much of realism, and too much of so-called 'truth' . . . We were struck by a thirst for dreams, for emotion, for poetry. Satiated with light too vivid and too crude, we longed for mists and fog. It was at this point that we attached ourselves passionately to the poetic and misty art of Puvis de Chavannes. We even admired its worst mistakes, its faulty draughtsmanship, its anaemic colours, so weary were we of admiring in other painters what we took to be good drawing and colour. Thus the art of Puvis de Chavannes became for us something like a cure; we clung to it as a patient clings to a new treatment.

The Nabis, Bernard, Signac, Gauguin and Matisse all found some element of inspiration in the work of an artist who was firmly wedded to the establishment, described a poem written to him by Mallarmé as 'an insanity' and firmly rejected overtures by younger artists to participate in their exhibitions. The secret of Puvis de Chavannes's appeal was that from the start of his career he had been concerned not so much with vision as with feeling, searching for some way to translate into plastic form the emotion he felt, as he himself put it:

A work of art emanates from a kind of confused emotion as an animal contained in its egg. I meditate upon the thought buried in this emotion until it appears as lucidly and distinctly as possible before my eyes.

21 Puvis de Chavannes
The Sacred Grove 1884

The Impressionists had evolved a technique of a novel kind for fulfilling a function which they shared with traditional painters, the accurate rendition of natural phenomena, but they had transferred this realization from the conceptual to the perceptual, not to express but to describe, painting what they actually saw, not what they thought they saw. But they had no very clear preconceptions of what to paint, beyond a rather vague commitment to realism and contemporary life and the avoidance of any subject – religious, historic, literary or patriotic – which added another dimension to that of pure vision. In this they differed from Courbet who in his manner of painting and in his images of people was realist but who beyond that produced very few Realist pictures. He never painted railway stations, boulevards, brothels, markets, dancing halls, circuses or boating parties. The Impressionists' concern with 'the heroism of modern life' was partly foisted on them by Zola (Realism was

34

basically and in the public eye more prestigiously a literary movement) and partly assumed because it was in the air and provided a ready-made platform. The generation which was following them demanded something else. They were discontented with what had become a dialogue between the painter and nature and yearned for an art which involved the personalities of the spectators, arousing in them a response conditioned by an appropriate arrangement of emotive colours and lines, or equally by emotive images linked with some other non-aesthetic mode of experience. At the same time, too, they were almost equally concerned that mere subjective responses on the part of artists should not be the sole touchstone of the artists' achievements and that they should be able to present a vindication of their work either in terms of a structural syntax or an ideological framework. But to do either they must reach the public and have their works exhibited.

22 Bonnard *France-Champagne* 1889, poster

CHAPTER TWO

The End of an Old World

Ever since the notion of two kinds of art, one official, the other revolutionary, had become tacitly accepted in the first half of the century the problem which increasingly exercised French artists who had no access to the annual Salon was where to exhibit. It was becoming more than ever obvious that some kind of regular public exposure was necessary to introduce new artists and new styles to the public and the critics, as well as to the dealers on whom their future would depend. The first and more famous of these, the Salon des Refusés of 1863, although in many ways a failure, had laid the foundation of Manet's reputation and enhanced that of Courbet and Whistler, as well as making clear to the public at large that there was an alternative to the art favoured by the Emperor, patronized by the State and bought by the *haute bourgeoisie*. It was this urge to find somewhere to exhibit a reasonably significant number of works which had led Manet and Courbet to mount their own exhibitions, just as much as it was the real motive behind a group of artists hiring a photographer's studio in the boulevard des Capucines and exhibiting their works to the public in April 1874. They saw it as a purely functional exercise, born out of frustration rather than defiance, and in a sense a response to the suggestion of Charles Blanc, the Minister of Fine Arts who, a year earlier after unsuccessful attempts to tinker with the administration of the Salon, had exclaimed 'Why don't artists start their own exhibition?'. The Impressionists had not been primarily concerned with creating a group or presenting a common style and emphasized the nature of their enterprise by forming themselves into a limited company with the commercially neutral title of La Société Anonyme des Peintres, Sculpteurs, Graveurs Etc. As Renoir later explained (recorded by Vollard in 1927),

I was afraid if the group were called 'The Somebodies' or 'The So-and-Sos', or even 'The Twenty Nine', the critics would start talking about a 'new school', when all that we were trying to do, within the limits of our abilities, was to try and induce painters in general to get in line and follow the masters, if they didn't want to see painting vanish without trace.

37

It was almost a fluke that certain of the exhibitors – who only contributed 54 of the 165 works on show – came to be called the 'Impressionists', thanks largely to the journalistic flair of the critic Louis Leroy.

The Impressionist exhibitions achieved results other than those connected with the emergence of a new style of painting. They confirmed the institutionalization of the notion of 'groups' in the art world. The Nazarenes in Rome and Germany, the Pre-Raphaelite Brotherhood in England and the Barbizon School in France had been forerunners of a phenomenon characterized by the breakdown of a central, generally accepted language of painting which had been predominant since the Renaissance. Henceforward sects would be characteristic of the art world and supplant any notion of a central aesthetic orthodoxy, each competing with and often supplanting others. The process was aggravated, as it had been with the Impressionists, by the need of critics and journalists and then of art historians, to impose easily understandable categories on what were often untidy phenomena. However, the names imposed on groups were often accepted with alacrity by their members as a successful form of public relations, and what might have started as a journalist's ploy could be converted into an aesthetic credo. During the twenty-five years after the last Impressionist exhibition there appeared Pointillism, the Pont-Aven School, Symbolism, Synthetism, Cloisonnism, Neo-traditionism, Divisionism, Traditionism, the Salon de la Rose + Croix, Fauvism, the Nabis. Outside France groups and movements proliferated: in Italy Divisionism, in Belgium the Libre Esthétique, in Holland Luminism, in Russia the Blue Rose, in Germany Die Brücke (the Bridge), in Sweden De Unga (the Young Ones) and in Britain Roger Fry's invention of the name Post-Impressionism was used to describe a number of groups ranging from the one that took its name from Fitzroy Street to that extensive and amorphous collection of artists centred around the adjoining but more salubrious locality of Bloomsbury.

This fragmentation of what had been the central body of beliefs of Impressionism was made possible, however, only through the development of an exhibition structure which had initially been the intention of those who participated in the boulevard des Capucines exhibition. It was through such exposure that doctrines could be developed, critical waters tested and the public made aware of new developments. Gauguin had been represented at five of the Impressionist exhibitions, starting in that of 1879; Seurat and Signac had managed to scrape into the last one with the support of Pissarro. But it was obvious in 1886 that the series had outlived its usefulness and that the founding fathers of the movement, having used these exhibitions to establish themselves, were now moving on to more lucrative forms of selling, more sophisticated publicity techniques. Two institutions soon appeared to fill the gap and to provide for the heirs of Impressionism, dissident or otherwise, the kind of exposure and publicity they needed.

In the course of 1883 a group of artists with little chance of having their works accepted by the Salon got together and founded the Groupe des Indépendants, the main purpose of which was to create an annual exhibition at which anyone prepared to pay a minimal fee could have their pictures hung without having to submit them to a jury. The first exhibition, held in an empty barracks in the Jardin des Tuileries, was a fiasco, even though the artists represented included Seurat, Signac and Redon. No accounts were kept, members of the executive committee fought each other and the police were constantly being brought in to restore order. After two days it closed but, thanks very largely to the efforts of Redon – who subsequently played an important part – the group was reconstituted as the Société des Artistes Indépendants, with a new constitution which stated: 'This Society stands for the suppression of juries and proposes to help artists freely to present their work before the bar of public opinion'. Artists were to be allowed to submit groups of their works, which would be hung together, a facility of which Redon took immediate advantage, exhibiting clusters of those charcoal drawings that became such an integral and significant part of his output. By 1886 when the Society had moved its venue to the Pavillon de la Ville in Paris, which had been constructed for the Universal Exhibition of 1878, Seurat, Signac 24 and their followers had a room devoted to themselves, a fact which made Gauguin reluctant to exhibit there. But he was exceptional; the Salon des Indépendants had become, and was to remain for some considerable time, a showcase for all the more progressive artists, including Guillaumin, Pissarro, Gauguin's subservient friend Schuf- fenecker, van Gogh (after his death Seurat arranged a small retrospective exhibition of his works there in 1891), Toulouse- 23 Lautrec, Cézanne and others. It certainly laid the foundations of Seurat's reputation. At the 1884 exhibition his *Baignade*, although it 5 was hung in the canteen, besides attracting Signac, caught the attention of Fénéon, who would write stimulatingly about the movement which he himself first called Neo-Impressionism.

In the same year that the Société des Artistes Indépendants was founded Brussels saw the establishment of another institution, which was to play an equally important part in publicizing and disseminating that cluster of innovative ideas in art which is described as Post-Impressionism. Belgium, linked to France by a common language and religion, had for most of its short national life been in close contact with Paris, especially as it was often the haven for political refugees. Durand-Ruel had established an art gallery there in 1871 and Impressionism had become widely accepted by the 1880s. Although there existed a forward-looking organization, the Société Libre des Beaux-Arts, the critics Octave Maus and Emile Verhaeren and the painter Théo van Rysselberghe founded a group known as Les Vingt, for the obvious reason that it had twenty members. It held the first of its projected annual exhibitions in February 1884. The group included artists as disparate as James Ensor, Jan Toorop, Henry van de Velde, Fernand Khnopff and older Barbizonesque figures such as Willem Vogels. It soon became apparent that the dominating

23 Toulouse-Lautrec *At the Cirque Fernando: Rider* 1888

24 Seurat *The Circus* 1890–91

25 personality in the group was the 31-year-old secretary Maus, a vibrant and dynamic character, who was to convert it into one of the most influential organizations on the European art scene. Not only did he introduce music and literature but he also insisted that each annual exhibition should include works by artists from other countries who were broadly in agreement with the attitudes of the group itself. In the course of the next few years Les Vingt included in its annual exhibition collections of works by Monet, Renoir, Pissarro, Seurat, Signac, Bracquemond, Rodin, Toulouse-Lautrec, Gauguin, Redon, van Gogh, Whistler, Cézanne, the German eccentric Max Klinger and the 'academic realist' Henri Gervex.

25 Van Rysselberghe *Portrait of Octave Maus* 1885

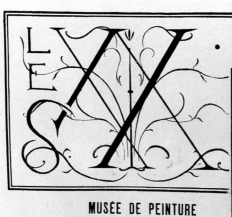

LE XX S

18 91.

MUSÉE DE PEINTURE
Place du Musée

VIIIe EXPOSITION

8 FÉVRIER-8 MARS

De 10 à 5 heures

Invités	Vingtistes
CHARLES ANGRAND	ANNA BOCH
JEAN BAFFIER	FRANTZ CHARLET
MAURITS BAUER	GUILLAUME CHARLIER
JULES CHÉRET	PAUL DUBOIS
WALTER CRANE	JAMES ENSOR
CHARLES FILLIGER	WILLY-A. FINCH
PAUL GAUGUIN	FERNAND KHNOPFF
ARMAND GUILLAUMIN	GEORGES LEMMEN
CARL LARSSON	GEORGES MINNE
ADOLF OBERLÆNDER	ROBERT PICARD
CAMILLE PISSARRO	DARIO DE REGOYOS
GEORGES SEURAT	AUGUSTE RODIN
A. SISLEY	FÉLICIEN ROPS
EUGÈNE SMITS	WILLY SCHLOBACH
P. WILSON STEER	PAUL SIGNAC
VINCENT VAN GOGH	JAN TOOROP
CHARLES VAN DER STAPPEN	HENRY VAN DE VELDE
FLORIS VERSTER	THÉO. VAN RYSSELBERGHE
	GUILL-S. VAN STRYDONCK
Belgique, France, Grande-Bretagne, Pays-Bas, Allemagne, Scandinavie	GUILLAUME VOGELS

BRUX ELLS

PRIX D'ENTRÉE : 5o CENTIMES

Cartes permanentes . . . . 15 francs
Donnant droit à l'entrée le jour de l'ouverture

Aux **CONCERTS** et **CONFÉRENCES** . . 2 francs

Le Trésorier.	Le Secrétaire.
Victor BERNIER	Octave MAUS

Fac-similé d'une affiche de M. F. KHNOPFF. (Mᵐᵉ Vᵉ Monnom, impr. à Bruxelles.)

26 Khnopff *Les XX* 1891, poster

44

27 Toulouse-Lautrec *Mlle Marcelle Lender* 1895, poster

28 Toulouse-Lautrec *Aristide Bruant dans son cabaret* 1892, poster

29 Mucha *Salon des Cent* 1896, poster

Les Vingt was the first serious attempt to create an international forum for the avant-garde and its success can be gauged from the results of the 1886 exhibition at which Seurat and Pissarro had been invited to participate. Signac, who attended the opening, wrote to Pissarro:

I have just left the exhibition exhausted. A huge crowd, a terrible throng, very bourgeois and anti-art. By and large it is a great success for us. Seurat's painting (*La Grande Jatte*) was practically invisible; the crowd in front of it was so large that it was impossible to get anywhere near it. The exhibition hall is a magnificent gallery in the museum [the Ancien Musée de Peinture], very large and with excellent light. It would be impossible to find anything better. Your paintings look very well, but unfortunately they are rather isolated because there are so few of them, and they are so comparatively small. However, the effect which has been produced has been quite significant. The pointillist technique intrigues visitors and makes them think. They realise that there must be something in it.

The impact of Seurat's great work was immediate. In February 1887 in *La Vie Moderne*, the main publication of the Belgian intelligentsia, Verhaeren wrote:

M. Seurat is derided as a chemist, a scientist, or something of that sort. But he uses his scientific technique only as a means of organizing his visual experience; they give him an added sense of certainty. What harm is there in this? *La Grande Jatte* is painted with a primitive simplicity and directness. In the same way the old masters, risking rigidity, arranged their figures in a hierarchic order, M. Seurat synthesizes attitudes, postures, movements. What the old masters did to express the values of their time he does for his, and he does it with the same exactitude, concentration and honesty. The gestures of the promenaders, the groups they form and their relation to each other could not be other than they are.

There were more tangible benefits for Seurat. Verhaeren acquired (possibly as a gift from the artist) *Lighthouse at Honfleur* and another buyer bought *Bec du Hoc* for 300 francs. More significantly, a number of members of Les Vingt were converted to Pointillism. These included Alfred William Finch, a painter of English parentage and a friend of Whistler, and Ensor, an exhibitor at the Salon des Indépendants who moved to Finland in 1897 and introduced the movement there; Van Rysselberghe, who was later to persuade the Fauves to exhibit in Brussels, and Van de Velde, who was to achieve later fame as a designer.

Les Vingt clearly introduced a formula for cross-fertilization of innovative ideas in the arts, with foreign participating artists

30 Seurat *Lighthouse at Honfleur* 1886

subsequently inviting members of the group to exhibit in their own
countries. This pattern survived the existence of Les Vingt as a group –
in 1893 it was transformed into La Libre Esthétique. The change in
title was relevant, quite apart from its connection with the English
Aesthetic movement, for it signalled a new link with the decorative
arts that had first become apparent in the last two exhibitions of Les
Vingt in 1891 and 1893 which had included two vases, a statuette and
two sculpted wood panels by Gauguin, a screen by Bernard and
cartoons for eight stained-glass windows by Paul Albert Besnard,
illustrations by Walter Crane and craft work by Van de Velde, who
was greatly influenced by the teachings of William Morris and Finch.

31 Rousseau *La Charmeuse de serpents* 1907

The Libre Esthétique increased this connection between art and craft and presented an opportunity for the Arts and Crafts movement, which had largely grown up in England, to come into contact with the non-naturalist, non-ideological work of the Parisian decorative tradition and thus open up the most spectacular episode in the history 29 of Art Nouveau. This connection was endemic to Post-Impressionism generally; Toulouse-Lautrec, who in addition to his posters, 27, 28 illustrations and prints also designed a stained-glass window for Tiffany's of New York, was one of the more outstanding examples, the Omega workshops of Fry and the Bloomsburyites one of the best-intentioned, but many of the artists involved in the new trends produced screens, fans, textiles and sculpted objects of one kind or another, as well as a more extensive amount of graphic work than any other comparable artistic movement of the past.

The same inclination to the decorative arts was also apparent in yet another Parisian experiment, the Société Nationale des Beaux-Arts, closer in feeling to the Salon, which had been founded in 1891 by Puvis de Chavannes, Rodin, Carrière and Meissonier and which included amongst its members Carolus-Duran, Sargent and Boldini. An immediate success, its first exhibition netted 170,000 francs in admission fees. It was more open-minded than the names of its members might suggest. Some weeks before it opened, Gauguin reported to his wife:

Meissonier's group will open this year a section of sculptural art. Yesterday I received an emissary from these gentlemen, the son of Renan, who had been commissioned especially to invite me to exhibit my ceramics and my wood sculptures. As I am almost the only one who does work of this kind or, in any case, the strongest and the one who receives most attention.

The invitation was all the more remarkable in that Gauguin's wooden bas-relief sculptures, which he had been doing for the past three years, were variously described as 'pornographic images of sublime ignorance' and products of 'the erotic and macabre temperament of a genius of lewdness, a dilettante of infamy, who is haunted by vice'. They were, however, symbolic or could be seen as such and, with artists such as Carrière and Puvis de Chavannes playing a significant role in the Société des Beaux-Arts, it can be seen that it would easily become a haven for those artists that way inclined.

If the Salon des Indépendants provided a showcase for the rebels who were reacting against Impressionism, the Salon d'Automne did the same for its later and more violent expressions. The idea for yet another Salon seems to have come from the curiously forenamed Yvanhoé Ramsbosson, a curator at the museum of the Petit Palais which housed the art collections of the city of Paris. He was able to make the museum available as a site for annual exhibitions, timed, unlike all the others, to open in the autumn. The first president was Frantz Jourdain, an architect and president of an art critics' association who, despite his many irritating faults, was a vigorous defender of new modes of expression and later gave the Cubists space when others would have excluded them. In 1903 Carrière became an honorary vice-president and two years later Renoir. Amongst the first to join were Rouault, Vuillard, Félix Vallotton and the portraitist Antonio de la Gandara. The great merit of the Salon d'Automne was its catholic quality, showing as it did works by very different kinds of artists. In 1903 it presented a small posthumous tribute to Gauguin, who had died in May; in the following year there were special exhibitions devoted to Puvis de Chavannes and Cézanne. The Salon also had special sections for posters, design and illustrations, included poets and writers amongst its members and, as with Les Vingt, promoted concerts.

The most spectacular exhibition of the Salon d'Automne took place in 1905, when the 'special' displays were devoted to Ingres and Manet, as if to underline the revolutionary quality of the contemporary works on the walls. This indeed was quite deliberate, as Elie Faure pointed out in his introduction to the catalogue:

The Salon d'Automne has undertaken to demonstrate, by its retrospective exhibitions, the permanent right of revolutionary endeavour to rejoin tradition. Like Puvis last year, Ingres and Manet make us aware that the revolutionary of today is the classic of tomorrow.

Much more than any other exhibition, and certainly more so than Roger Fry's hotchpotch at the Grafton Galleries in 1910, the 1905 Salon d'Automne, which had transferred its venue from the Petit to the Grand Palais, was an almost complete display of all that Post-Impressionism meant. The *pièce de résistance*, which had an impact almost comparable to that provoked by Manet's *Déjeuner sur l'herbe* of 1863, was Matisse's *Woman with a Hat*. In its violence of colour, its Cézanne-like solidity, it presaged the advent of the Fauves, the most dedicated exponents of the colourist as opposed to the linear traditions of the Impressionists. The reactions of the Steins were typical. Leo, who had bought Cézanne's *Portrait of Madame Cézanne*, wrote in his *Journey into the Self*:

It was a tremendous effort on his part, a thing brilliant and powerful, but the nastiest smear of paint I had ever seen. It was what I was unknowingly waiting for, and I would have snatched it at once if I had not needed a few days to get over the unpleasantness of the putting on of paint. One was not yet accustomed to the smears that since then are commonplaces of technique.

Gertrude's reactions were quite different, as she wrote in *The Autobiography of Alice B. Toklas*:

People were roaring with laughter at the picture and scratching at it. Gertrude Stein could not understand why, the picture seemed to her perfectly natural. The Cézanne portrait had not seemed natural, it had taken her some time to feel that it was natural, but this picture by Matisse seemed perfectly natural. Her brother was less attracted, but all the same they bought it. She then went back to look at it again and it upset her to see them all mocking it. It bothered her and angered her because she did not understand why because to her it was all right.

The didactic element implicit in the Salon d'Automne exhibitions was emphasized by the hanging. *Woman with a Hat* was hung, with nine other works by Matisse, in Room Seven, along with paintings by Derain, Vlaminck, Marquet, van Dongen, Friesz and Louis Valtat. The exhibition also hung works by the Impressionists – including several Renoirs, ten paintings by Cézanne and paintings by 33 Guillaumin, Redon and Raffaëlli. The sculpture consisted of works by Rodin, Bourdelle, Rembrandt Bugatti, Maillol and Albert Marque, whose statue of a young boy in Room Seven prompted the critic Louis Vauxcelles to remark, 'Ah Donatello parmi les fauves' (Donatello amongst the wild beasts), thus giving the group its name. What might be thought of as the mainstream Post-Impressionists were represented by Bonnard, Vuillard, Vallotton and Ker-Xavier Roussel. An enormous painting (over 2 × 3 metres) by the Douanier Rousseau dominated Room Seven. It was entitled 'Le lion ayant 34 faim, se jette sur l'antelope, la dévore, la panthère attend avec anxiété le moment ou elle aussi, pourra en avoir sa part. Des oiseaux carnivores ont déhiqueté chacun un morceau de chair de dessus le pauvre animal, versant un pleur. Soleil couchant'. (The hungry lion leaps on the antelope and devours it. The panther awaits anxiously for the moment when it too can have its share. Some carnivorous birds have each torn a piece from the poor animal, who is shedding a tear. Setting sun.) The presence of this entirely unexpected work from a 60-year-old customs officer was an indication of how comprehensively the exhibition covered every aspect of French painting in the 31 opening years of the twentieth century.

51

32 *L'Illustration* 4 November
1905, on the Salon d'Automne

33 Cézanne
Bathers Resting 1876–7

34 Rousseau
The Hungry Lion . . . 1905

It put in their appropriate context not only Impressionism and its enemies but also those other artists whose reactions against it constituted the dominant elements of Post-Impressionism and some of whom, such as Rouault, Kandinsky, Jawlensky and Picabia, were to take painting into as yet unknown regions.

There was amongst the public as a whole by the end of the century a far more tolerant attitude to modern art than had existed at the time of the first Impressionist exhibition in 1874. The publicly displayed posters of artists such as Jules Chéret, Toulouse-Lautrec and Steinlen, the proliferation of books, magazines and ephemera illustrated by 'advanced' artists (the Salon d'Automne displayed music sheets with covers by Bonnard and Chéret) and an increasing visual awareness stimulated by improved art education had broken down many of the prejudices which an earlier generation of innovators had had to fight. This was reflected in the development of a whole range of novel outlets for artists anxious to display to the public their own new styles. Typical of these were the many bars, cafés and cabarets of Montmartre, which since the 1880s had been developing into an artistic colony. Most of them had either a permanent exhibition of paintings or else mounted exhibitions by specific artists.

36

35, 37
38, 39
40

Au Bal du « Courrier Français ». à l'Elysée Montmartre. Dessin de MARTIN GÉDDAN.

35 *Medieval Ball at l'Elysée Montmartre*, from *Le Courrier Français* 1893

36 The first woman bill-poster in Paris

37 Luce *View of Montmartre* 1887

38 L. Pissarro *Soup* (the Café Nouvelles-Athènes or the Café Volpini) 1889

39 Seurat *Eden Concert* 1887–8

40 Bonnard
The Cab-horse, c. 1895

Men such as Aristide Bruant, immortalized by Toulouse-Lautrec, whose works he did so much to promote, made his two *cabarets artistiques*, the Chat Noir and Le Mirliton into virtual art centres which by showing innovative artists at early stages in their careers made them initially free of the usual exhibition machinery. Van Gogh in 1887 discovered in the Café Tambourin on the boulevard Clichy a friendly proprietor, La Segatori, an erstwhile artists' model, who allowed him to stage an exhibition there of works by himself, Anquetin, Bernard and Lautrec. He also did some paintings for the interior of the café but these the subsequent proprietor refused to return and they have disappeared. The place was frequented by a number of artists and writers, including Ernest Hoschedé, one-time proprietor of a department store and a patron of Monet, at whose house in Giverny his wife and children were living. Very soon, however, complications arose between van Gogh and La Segatori and the exhibition closed without any sales. Still, his paintings had been seen.

A more ambitious café experiment was launched in 1889, as an admittedly puny gesture against the Fine Arts Section of the fourth Universal Exhibition which was being held in the Champs de Mars under the shadow of the newly built Eiffel Tower and which attracted some thirty-three million visitors. Next to the official art sections was the Café des Arts which boasted a large, newly built hall, planned to be covered on the interior with mirrors which hadn't arrived. Gauguin's friend Schuffenecker persuaded the owner, a Signor Volpini, to allow the walls to be covered with red canvas and to hang there an exhibition that was originally intended to consist of some 50 paintings but in the end included 100 paintings, drawings and watercolours by Gauguin, Schuffenecker, Bernard, Charles Laval,

EXPOSANTS

Paul Gauguin	E. Schuffenecker	Emile Bernard
Charles Laval	Louis Anquetin	Louis Roy
Léon Fauché	Georges Daniel	Ludovic Nemo

42 Anquetin *Avenue de Clichy, 5 O'clock in the Evening* 1887

41 Gauguin *Aux Roches noires*, frontispiece of the Volpini exhibition catalogue, 1889

Émile Fauché, Anquetin, Louis Roy and Daniel de Monfreid. Two artists who were invited to exhibit but refused were Guillaumin and van Gogh. The latter wrote in June 1889 to his brother, who had been responsible for declining the invitation:

I think you are right not to show any of my pictures at the exhibition of Gauguin and the others, and there is a valid reason for my abstaining without offending them, as long as I myself am not completely cured. For me there is no question that Bernard and Gauguin have real and great merit. But it is very understandable that for men like them who are very much alive and young, and who must live and try and get ahead, it is impossible to turn their canvases against the wall until it pleases other people to admit them into the official hotchpotch. By showing in cafés one may cause a sensation which, I don't deny it, may be in bad taste, but I myself may have the same crime on my conscience, having exhibited at the Tambourin. I am therefore more to blame than they are, as far as causing a sensation is concerned, though heaven only knows I did it unintentionally. Young Bernard, in my opinion, has already painted some astonishing canvases in which there is a gentleness and something essentially French of rare quality. Anyway neither he nor Gauguin is an artist who could possibly give the impression of trying to enter the World's Fair through the service entrance. You may be sure of that. It is understandable that they *could not* keep quiet.

The exhibition was advertised in red, white and blue posters and was described by a title, 'Groupe Impressionniste et Synthétiste', that had been invented by Gauguin himself and indicated the extent to which he still saw himself and the group as part of the Impressionist tradition. More interestingly, however, in view of the fact that most of the paintings were of Breton subjects, it came to be seen as the first public manifestation of the Pont-Aven group. Although disregarded by the general press, the exhibition received a fair amount of publicity in Symbolist and other avant-garde publications. Fénéon commented on the fact that Gauguin, like Seurat, was concerned with creating 'an art of synthesis and premeditation' but used different means:

reality for him is only a pretext for far-reaching creations; he re-arranges the materials reality provides, disdains illusionist effects, even atmospheric ones; accentuates lines, limits their number, makes them hieratic, and in each of the spacious areas formed by their interlacing, an opulent and sultry colour sits in bleak glory, without impinging on neighbouring colours, without yielding its own tone.

Several critics, however, paid more attention to 'the bosom of M. Volpini's cashier' and the delights of an orchestra of dubious Russian female violinists, accompanied by a single male cornet player.

Van Gogh had very acutely described the merits and de-merits of café exhibitions, but there were other outlets for painters working in that spectrum of styles absorbed into the generic grouping of Post-Impressionism, who lacked either the contacts or the stylistic adaptability to get into any of the official Salons. One of the most curious of these was the Salon de la Rose + Croix, held yearly at 44 Durand-Ruel's from 1892 to 1897. This was the brain-child of the curious Sâr Mérodack Joséphin Péladan, poet, journalist, entrepre 43 neur and the leader of a quasi-Catholic revivalist group financed by a dilettante painter, the Comte Antoine de la Rochefoucauld (*see* Chapter 5). Péladan's theories were a mixture of neo-Scholasticism, occultism and Symbolism and he restricted entries to his exhibitions purely by the subject matter of the works. He proscribed any concerned with modern life, war, naturalistic landscapes and portraiture but welcomed anything allegorical, medieval, lyrical or mystical. The curious thing is that the two most famous exponents of this kind of art, Puvis de Chavannes and Denis, did not participate in any of these exhibitions, which were largely composed of minor Symbolists. On the other hand, mainly because of la Rochefoucauld's connections, they did much to publicize the existence of a 'new art'.

None of the Post-Impressionist movements was powered by a dealer with the acumen and drive which Durand-Ruel had put at the disposal of the Impressionists. Ambroise Vollard was still a young 45 man in the closing years of the century, and his golden period was to come with the Cubists and their successors, but he was very active in promoting and selling the works of Cézanne. Late in 1895 he organized a one-man show of his paintings with considerable success, which led the young Henri Matisse to buy his *Three Bathers*. Vollard had first seen Cézanne's works at the shop of Père Tanguy, a colour 46 merchant in the rue Clauzel. An ex-Communard who first came into contact with avant-garde art through Pissarro, who bought his colours from him and with whom he shared political ideas, Tanguy started selling paintings and showing them in the window of his shop. He had close relations with van Gogh, who painted portraits of him and his wife, and for some considerable time had been the only dealer to sell the works of Cézanne, for which he charged between 80 and 100 francs. Other artists whose works he sold, in addition to Pissarro and Guillaumin, were Gauguin, Seurat, Signac (who bought one of Cézanne's works from him) and several of their followers. His shop in fact became the closest to a permanent exhibition centre that certain sections of the modern movement possessed.

43 Desboutin *Sâr Péladan* 1891

44 Schwabe *Salon de la Rose + Croix*
1892, poster

45 Cézanne *Portrait of A. Vollard* 1899

46 Bernard *Portrait of Père Tanguy* 1887

It was inevitable that Théo van Gogh after the arrival of his brother in Paris in 1886 should have extended the interest he had shown in the Impressionists as manager of Boussod & Valadon's to their successors. He started stocking works by his brother, by Pissarro, who was then going through his Pointillist style, and by Gauguin, but unfortunately he died before being able to continue. His successor, Maurice Joyant, continued with Gauguin, seventeen of whose works he sold between 1887 and 1891, as well as Redon and Toulouse-Lautrec.

Much more deeply involved in the whole gamut of Post-Impressionist art was the extrovert Le Barc de Boutteville, who had started his commercial career selling Old Masters but who, according to a notice by G. Albert which appeared in the *Mercure de France* in February 1892, had decided 'to offer a permanent shelter to the young artists, the innovators, who are still opposed by the critics, disdained by the customers and generally scoffed at by the dealers and juries'. The gallery in the rue Peletier was small, but Le Barc de Boutteville lived up to his promise and organized a series of exhibitions of 'Peintres Impressionniste et Symbolistes' that made it one of the centres of Parisian cultural life. The first included works by Anquetin, Bernard, Lautrec, Denis and Bonnard. The reception of the show was generally favourable and a lengthy article in the *Écho de Paris* included interviews with all the exhibitors, some of whom made illuminating remarks about their attitudes. Anquetin claimed 'Impressionism and Symbolism are only jokes; I care for no schools, no theories. Only temperament counts'; Toulouse-Lautrec repeated these sentiments, adding 'I work in my corner; I admire Degas and Forain.' Bernard emphasized his religious beliefs and opted for Cézanne and Redon as his favourite painters; Bonnard said that he too didn't belong to any school or group and that 'painting should be mainly decorative', sentiments echoed by Denis, who added 'We are not pretentious people, living with the conviction that we have discovered the definitive Art.'

Some critics commented on de Boutteville's irritating loquacity, the smallness of the gallery and the confusion of the hanging, but the success of the exhibitions is attested by the fact that 15 were held, each containing about 140 works. The catalogues had prefaces by a well-known writer or critic expressing often enough in language of histrionic intensity notions in flat contradiction to those expressed by the artists themselves. Here, for instance, is the Symbolist poet Camille Mauclair in the catalogue of the 1893 exhibition expatiating on the participating artists:

They are prophets. They proclaim the power of the human faculties. They have only marginal relationships with society, because they are a society unto themselves. They make no claim to material rewards, and see their honour as lying in the esteem in which they hold themselves in their isolation. Here we find a brotherly union between the sharpened vision of life and the idealized domination of that same life motivated by a common desire to take the plastic and visual laws that were given new life by the masters twenty years ago and put them in the service of providing new expressions of the human soul.

There can be no doubt that de Boutteville's exhibitions did spread the esteem in which the exhibitors were held by the art-loving public, however much they may have disliked the fact, and they were especially useful for Bonnard, Vuillard, Denis and Bernard who, in 1892, organized there a small – and unsuccessful – exhibition of sixteen paintings by van Gogh.

The graphic arts had been experiencing a massive revival in the last two decades of the nineteenth century, prompted partly by new developments in printing and reproduction processes, partly by the growth of the Arts and Crafts movement. Whereas, with the exception of Pissarro, reproductive processes had played little part in the work of the Impressionists, they did play an important and significant role in that of their immediate successors, offering a not inconsiderable income, ensuring wide publicity and most importantly accustoming people to their individual styles. The outstanding example is Toulouse-Lautrec who, in the course of a working life of some sixteen years, produced 368 prints and posters (in addition to 737 oil paintings, 275 watercolours and more than 5000 drawings). A diligent and painstaking craftsman, he greatly extended the range and subtleties of graphic reproduction and created precedents that were followed by Bonnard, Vuillard, Mucha, Steinlen, Munch, Matisse 22, 29 and countless others. Print sellers such as Sagot published regular 101 catalogues of prints and posters – the latter selling at between 2 and 12 francs. Prints were sold in limited editions, or printed on special kinds of paper at elevated prices. In 1897 Gustave Pellet, for instance, was selling prints of Toulouse-Lautrec's *La Loge* at 60 francs each and, at a time when the artist was being paid between 200 and 500 francs for his paintings, he received 800 francs from the English publisher Sands for eight drawings of Yvette Guilbert to be reproduced as lithographs.

Fénéon described Chéret, the originator of that magnificent style of French poster art which decorated Paris during the 'belle epoque', as 'the Tiepolo of the streets', and the range of public apprehension of

67

47 Denis *La Dépêche de Toulouse*
1892?, poster

new art styles was greatly enlarged by the fact that people accepted willingly in graphic art innovations which they would reject in art galleries or museums. Artists responded to this with a newly acquired
47 stylistic courage. Strongly influenced by Japanese prints, exploiting still further the visual vocabulary of Toulouse-Lautrec, encouraged
105 by the patronage of the magazine *La Revue Blanche*, Bonnard and
109, 113 Vuillard, especially in the 1890s, produced a large number of posters,
120 book illustrations, theatre programmes, albums and straightforward prints that in their use of flat colours and structured compositions greatly influenced their subsequent artistic developments and,
62 especially in the case of Vuillard, could not altogether unfancifully be described as anticipations of abstract art.

68

Print-making of different kinds was often undertaken for more ideological motives, on the assumption that it made art more easily available to the working classes – a notion especially attractive to the two Pissarros, Lucien establishing near London the Eragny Press which produced booklets illustrated with coloured engravings. Other artists had more private aims. Theo van Gogh had been the first to encourage Gauguin to turn his attention to print-making and his already well-established interest in wood-carving inclined him to engraving. Bernard, who had previously done a number of wood-engravings, discovered the potential of zincography in 1887 and taught the process to Gauguin, who produced eleven prints, which were announced in the Volpini exhibition catalogue and were intended as a kind of prospectus of the sort of work he could produce. Printed on brilliant yellow paper, they displayed a simplicity of outline which owed more than a little to the popular imagery of the *images d'Epinal* (*see* Chapter 4) and exploited the grainy effects of zinc – as opposed to the smoother texture of Bavarian stone – to produce a whole range of nuances in black and white. This was in effect part of a wider reaction amongst artists, who were coming to revolt against the industrialization of the image produced by mass-circulation magazines such as *L'Illustration* and *Le Rire*. Even van Gogh, who had originally derived so much pleasure and, indeed, inspiration from the pages of *The Graphic*, had written to his brother in 1882 about the illustrations in Charpentier's avant-garde magazine *La Vie Moderne*:

Much as I like these drawings, still there is something mechanical in them, something of the photograph or photogravure, and I prefer an ordinary lithograph by Daumier or Gavarni . . . I am afraid that a new process is one of those things which cannot quite satisfy me; they are usually too smooth. I mean that an ordinary etching, wood engraving or lithograph has a charm of originality which cannot be replaced by anything mechanical.

This new attitude, this quest for a kind of rugged, stylistic originality, had been marked by the founding in 1888 by Félix Bracquemond, a pillar of the Impressionist establishment and the person who had first interested Gauguin in ceramics, of *L'Estampe Originale*. It developed into the Société des Peintres-Graveur and published an album of individual artists' prints, which had a considerable success and was sold out by the end of the following year. The society also started a series of annual exhibitions, the first of which opened at Durand-Ruel's on the rue Peletier on 23 January 1889 and contained works by Degas, Pissarro, Redon, Bracquemond and Rodin – a prolific and versatile etcher.

With an organization such as this and the stimulus of regular exhibitions, it was not to be wondered at that print-making became an attractive outlet for nearly all the younger experimentalists. Bernard himself, unlike Gauguin, coloured his prints with water-colour and confined his subject matter very much to Brittany. All the artists associated with Gauguin and Pont-Aven became enthusiastic print-makers and members of the Société des Peintres-Graveur. Even Sérusier, who was passionately concerned with colour as a determinant factor in his work and was therefore disinclined to the merely graphic, produced a number either for sale in Paris or as illustrations to theatre programmes. Roderick O'Connor, who did not meet Gauguin till 1894, absorbed from him the principles of Synthetism, but in his etchings (he produced only one lithograph) exhibited a linear dynamism that went beyond it and displayed an Expressionist fervour which has affinities with the graphic work of Munch. Maxime Maufra too used his prints to arouse emotions other than the merely contemplative. As Claude Roger-Marx wrote in his intro-duction to the first *L'Estampe Originale* album:

It would seem impossible to come across anything that proclaims so vigorously the animating power of the human spirit. Take an inanimate piece of copper or stone. An artist comes along and in an instant makes this inert and lifeless matter palpitate, giving it life and thought. Meaningless yesterday, it now and for ever reveals a character, reflects a temperament, and discloses the very soul of the print-maker.

Gauguin himself, apart from an important etching of Mallarmé published in 1891 in an edition of about twelve impressions – printed on a variety of supports and clearly reflecting the influence of van Gogh's similar portrait of Dr Gachet etched in the previous year – did little more in this medium apart from a number of lithographs produced around 1889, mainly of subjects from Martinique. His

48 Redon *Portrait of Paul Sérusier* 1903

49 Redon *Portrait of Maurice Denis* 1903

50 Redon *Portrait of Pierre Bonnard* 1902

greatest achievements were to come a few years later when he reverted to his original penchant for wood-engraving and produced some on Tahitian themes. Ten appeared as illustrations, together with watercolour sketches in *Noa Noa*, the journal of his experiences as a painter in Tahiti, the text of which was written in collaboration with Charles Morice in 1893. These engravings were remarkable in many ways. They pioneered the application to the graphic arts of what had originally been a Ruskinian principle – but which was to dominate much artistic thinking for the next half-century – of conforming to the demands of the nature of the material used, thus achieving in this particular case a kind of ferocious simplicity, imposed by the relative intractability of the wood. This in itself gave the resultant imagery an emotional intensity which was later to influence the works of Expressionists such as Karl Schmidt-Rottluff and Erich Heckel. It provided as well a reading of the human face and figure which linked with African primitivism to give Picasso the figurative idiom that he exploited in works such as *Les Demoiselles d'Avignon* and that became the accepted anatomical idiom of most 'modernist' art.

The many-faceted nature of Post-Impressionism was made possible by the increase in the number of smaller art galleries prepared to exhibit works of a more explorative kind and by the creation of exhibiting organizations dedicated to a more catholic standard of selection than that which had marked official bodies such as the Salon. Its innovative qualities had been made acceptable to a wider public by the posters of artists such as Toulouse-Lautrec and Bonnard. The development of print-making as a viable and often commercially successful form of expression had not only enlarged its market but also enabled artists to carry out experiments in the use of colour and the more adventurous manipulation of line and contour which could be digested into their complete stylistic syntax.

51 Gauguin *Idole à la perle* 1892–3

CHAPTER THREE

Discovering New Worlds

Since the end of the Middle Ages, Europe had paid little or no
attention to cultures outside its own geographical boundaries and
subscribed, without any significant deviation, to the ideals and
standards of Graeco-Roman civilization, with the various modifica-
tions imposed by Christianity. From the seventeenth century
onwards the decorative arts, and to a lesser extent architecture, had
reflected some Chinese and Japanese influences – the two were
indistinguishable from each other to Europeans at the time. But when
Napoleon invaded Egypt in 1798 he was accompanied by a troupe of
scholars and artists whose labours revealed in greater detail and with
more extensive illustration the richness of a culture which had
previously been regarded as little more than the background to Old
Testament villains and nubile queens. Here again the direct influences
were at first purely architectural and decorative. With the expansion
of colonialism, as the outer world was gradually revealed to
Europeans in the nineteenth century by the efforts of soldiers,
missionaries and traders, artists saw it first merely as a source of
inspirational landscapes and picturesque bric-à-brac. When Delacroix
visited recently opened-up Morocco in 1823 in the entourage of the
Comte de Mornay, he produced some remarkable paintings but
seems to have been oblivious of and untouched by any aspect of
Islamic art. Some sixty years later Renoir was to confess to the
influence which his visits to Algeria had exerted on him but he was
talking about the effects of strong light on the resultant shadows
rather than any aesthetic experience.

It was not until the 1860s that European painters began to be
directly influenced by a style and an artistic tradition almost entirely
outside the humanistic tradition of the Renaissance to which they had
for so long been devoted. When Commodore Perry's gunships
opened up the trade of Japan to the outer world in 1854, they were, no
doubt unwittingly, releasing on Europe an artistic influence of an
extent which it had not experienced since the early Middle Ages.
France was especially receptive to this onslaught. Emporia such as the

52 Hokusai, 'The Goddess Konohana
Sakuya Hime', no. 1 from *One
Hundred Views of Mount Fuji* 1830s

Porte Chinoise and the more sophisticated gallery of the dealer
Samuel Bing and his adviser Tadamasa Hayashi did a roaring trade
and became the social centres of cultural life in Paris. A club, the
Jinglar, was founded where members wore kimonos and ate with
chopsticks off tableware decorated with designs by Katsushika
52 Hokusai and Ando Hiroshige. The tableware was by Félix Bracquemond, who was to be a regular contributor to the Impressionist
exhibitions. Books about Japan proliferated and at the Universal
Exhibitions of 1867 and 1878 the considerable Japanese presence
spread amongst the general public a wider realization of the artistic
achievements in design and print-making of the Heavenly Kingdom.

No artist's studio was complete without its stock of kimonos, fans
and appropriate ceramics. But only the Impressionists, especially
Manet, Degas, Monet and Mary Cassatt, absorbed into their own
work compositional devices, points of view and perspectival tricks
and approaches to the use of colour which had been commonplace in
Japanese art a century earlier. However, most of the Impressionists

74

53 Van Gogh *Japonaiserie: Oiran* 1887

54 Le Japon, cover of *Paris Illustré*
May 1866

55 Van Gogh *La Segatori au Café
Tambourin* 1887

were restrained in their adaptation of such influences by their own overriding concern with the depiction of the evanescent effects of light and with a spontaneous reaction to nature which was peculiar to their own artistic ethos. Such inhibitions did not bother their successors and the art of the Japanese print – especially the woodcut – produced one of the dominant characteristics of Post-Impressionism.

Van Gogh had first discovered Japanese prints in Antwerp. His 53, 54 enthusiasm for them grew in Paris, where he spent hours at Bing's, and in 1887 he arranged an exhibition of them in collaboration with Théo at Le Tambourin – he painted some in the background of his 55, 66 painting of La Segatori. Japanese prints also appeared in his portrait of Père Tanguy (1887–8), who always kept a supply of them in his shop. Van Gogh copied several of them, including Hiroshige's *Ohashi Bridge in Rain*, with characteristic vivacity and a considerable degree of accuracy. When he decided to move to the south, he described Provence as 'a second Japan' and as soon as he arrived at Arles in 1888 he hung coloured wood-engravings by his favourite Japanese artists on the walls of his room in the Yellow House. In September he wrote to Théo:

I envy the Japanese the extreme clearness which everything has in their work. It is never wearisome and never seems to be done too hurriedly. Their work is as simple as breathing, and they do a figure in a few sure strokes with the same ease as if it were buttoning your waistcoat.

It was this spontaneous clarity and simplicity of Japanese prints which also appealed so strongly to Vallotton and Bernard, both of whom had become involved in wood-engraving by the 1890s, and to Gauguin. Influenced by the use of bold, flat colours and emphatic, sinuous lines, he also incorporated Japanese motifs such as *netsuke* figures into his carvings (*see* pp. 94–5). He included Japanese prints in several of his paintings, such as his portrait of the Schuffenecker family and the *Still Life with Head-shaped Vase and Japanese Woodcut*, both of 65 1889. The figure of Jacob in *The Vision after the Sermon: The Struggle of Jacob and the Angel* is derived from Hokusai's *Manga* and in his 94 lithographs from Martinique, as well as in his illustrations to *Noa Noa*, Gauguin drew extensively on the vocabulary of Japanese pictorial conventions to represent phenomena such as waves. After his death, amongst the meagre possessions of his sold by auction were two triptychs, Kunichika's *Wrestlers* and Kunifuku's *Eagle with a Bear in its Talons*, both exercises in that kind of pictorial vigour so characteristic of his own work.

The formalized stances and the hieratic quality which appear in so many of the paintings of both Seurat and Signac are clearly related to their shared passion for Japanese art. It was enthusiastically promoted by the ever-explorative Fénéon who planned, but did not realize, a book on the subject. His remarks on the theme were always acute and show an intimate awareness of techniques involved in print-making and the characteristics of the different artists. Reviewing an exhibition of Mary Cassatt's works, for instance, he wrote: 56

She may take what she wants from the [Japanese] tradition, provided she keeps her originality intact. She should generalize her interest rather than emulate. Today the way she makes a network of arms, shoulders, and generally all the lines of the nude remind one too much of dar Utamaro, and so show the influence of those chubby necks in Kiyonaga – although without the latter's facile, somewhat vulgar naturalism.

56 Cassatt *In the Omnibus* 1891

In 1883 the Georges Petit Gallery organized an exhibition of some three thousand Japanese works of art, predominantly prints and engravings, and five years later Bing started publishing a magazine, *Le Japon artistique*. A year later the Universal Exhibition, intended to celebrate the centenary of the Revolution, included the usual Japanese artefacts and a troupe of dancers led by Sada Yakko, which emphasized the contemporaneity of an artistic tradition which had often been seen merely as a historical curiosity. Official recognition followed commercial initiative. In 1879 the Guimet Collection, with its wealth of Far Eastern art, was moved from Lyons to Paris and in 1896 the renowned collector of Oriental art, Enrico Cernuschi, bequeathed to the City of Paris the treasures he had accumulated in his house in the Parc Monceau. The generation of students who were leaving the École des Beaux-Arts or the ateliers of teaching painters such as Cormon were being exposed to these non-European influences on an unprecedented scale. Typical of these young painters was the charismatic Anquetin, who dominated his generation at Cormon's atelier and became one of the leading lights of Bruant's Mirliton cabaret. He evolved, in collaboration with another pupil of Cormon, Bernard, a style which they called 'Cloisonnism', based primarily on Japanese prints with the addition of elements from medieval stained glass and the exploitation of flat areas of colour as in *cloisonné* enamelling, which provided them with their name. Anquetin combined this innovative style with a concern for depicting
42 the street and café life of Montmartre, which gave his works at this time a sense of startling modernity. But within six years of producing
57 works such as *Girl reading a Newspaper* he abandoned it all in favour of a kind of aetiolated Baroque, anticipating in this way the late career of De Chirico.

Toulouse-Lautrec's passion for things Japanese probably predated his meeting with Anquetin at Cormon's studio, and he certainly visited enthusiastically the Georges Petit exhibition of 1883. He bought several prints from Antoine Portier, who lived in the house where van Gogh was staying in the rue Lépic, and later from his friend Maurice Joyant, who had succeeded Théo van Gogh as the manager of the Montmartre branch of Goupil. Several of these are depicted pasted on a screen in his *Portrait of Rachou*. Like his father, he had a
58 passion for dressing up and frequently appears in photographs clad in *daimyo* robes. The influence on him of Japanese prints was far more profound than this would suggest. Lautrec had been brought up as a painter in the traditions of Impressionism but his own inclinations and

78

57 Anquetin *Girl reading a Newspaper* 1890

58 Toulouse-Lautrec in Japanese samurai costume, *c.* 1892

the circumstances of his own life impelled him to the production of posters and prints predominantly in colour lithography. A dedicated and pertinacious craftsman, he applied himself to understanding the technique and potentialities of this medium, which involved the use of separate blocks for each colour, superimposed on a key outline. Basically this was the same technique the Japanese had used for their coloured wood-engravings and Lautrec acquired from their example the stylistic mannerisms – flat colours, bold outlines, truncated edges, the abandonment of any suggestion of *chiaroscuro* and the use of complex combinations of colours – that made his graphic work so revolutionary. Whereas his predecessors in this field had used a comparatively simple range of colours, Lautrec not only evolved a very individual range of more complex shades but also experimented, as the Japanese had done, with other materials. When, for instance, Danjuro VII had produce some thirty years earlier a coloured engraving of an actor, he added to the colours a sprinkling of powdered brass and mica. When in 1893 Lautrec treated an analogous theme – the American dancer Loïe Fuller on the stage – he emphasized the primacy of her dress as Danjuro had done in his engraving and used a formidable combination of techniques. The basic drawing is in

59 Danjuro VII *Actor in a Shibaraku Role, c.* 1820

60 Toulouse-Lautrec *Miss Loïe Fuller* 1893, poster

various shades of olive green and blue on a reddish-brown tinted plate; Fuller's face and legs are of a light yellowish brown and her robe a shimmering mixture of red, violet, blue, yellow and green. The background is of various bronze tones, applied with a combination of brush and spraying techniques, whilst the whole has been dusted over with gold particles, applied with cotton pads. This is a work which can be seen as a microcosm of many of the most common elements to be found in so much Post-Impressionistic art: a concern with the decorative, a rejection of the tonal modulations and chromatic analysis of Impressionism and the use of expressive rather than descriptive colour. Firmly set in the iconography of contemporary life, Lautrec's lithographs not only influenced his own painting but also showed a public wider than that which visited the comparatively few galleries specializing in what a later generation would call 'experimental' art that styles were evolving which owed nothing to the academic tradition and precious little even to Impressionism.

A further impetus to the diffusion of the Japanese influence occurred in 1890 when the École des Beaux-Arts mounted an exhibition of nearly a thousand Ukiyo-e prints. This style had originally emerged in the sixteenth century to supply a popular market for imagery depicting contemporary urban life. It was designed to satisfy the tastes of the working and commercial classes and, although it included artists such as Hokusai and Hiroshige, its vitality had started to decline in Japan by the end of the nineteenth century. The exhibition had a particularly strong influence on the Nabis. Bonnard, for instance, who had already designed a lithograph poster for *France-Champagne* in a style that still had echoes of Chéret and Lautrec but in its treatment of broad, linear patterns suggested the influence of Hokusai, began to collect prints by Kuniyoshi, Hiroshige and Kunisada. Of these three, the most important influence was that of Hiroshige, especially evident in Bonnard's album of twelve 61 lithographs published in 1899 entitled *Quelques aspects de la vie de Paris*. It is full of animated figures scattered haphazardly over the surface of the print, without any central focal point, or arranged in a frieze around the edges of the paper. His enthusiasm for the art of Japan was so fervent that he was known as 'le Nabi très Japonard'. It dominated his paintings as well as his prints. His works at this period have virtually no suggestion of three-dimensional space and are formed of intricate patterns of silhouettes, arabesques and large areas of patterns; many assume extreme vertical or horizontal proportions – he was very involved in producing decorative panels. Like the Ukiyo-e print-makers he was deeply concerned with everyday life, the intimacies of personal contact frozen in a moment of recognition, not recorded in detailed analysis but expressed in simplified forms with flat colours, frolicsome lines and occasional eccentricities such as the use of velvet instead of canvas. Another characteristic of his work, shared by many of his contemporaries, was the diversity of his output. In addition to decorative panels he designed stained glass and furniture, as well as being an active book–illustrator and a stage-designer of considerable talent, working mainly for the Théâtre de l'Oeuvre, where he was responsible for the presentation of the young poet Alfred Jarry's *Ubu Roi* in 1896. Increasingly, however, Bonnard, like Roussel and Denis, Anquetin and others, yearned for the security of a tradition. Whereas they turned to various forms of classicism, he reverted to the tradition in which he had been brought up and spent the rest of his life painting successful and charming pictures which suggest a kind of Impressionism heavily modified by his intense contact with Japanese art and to a lesser extent by his short flirtation with the emotive colouring of the Fauves.

There is no documentary evidence about Vuillard's interest in Japanese art. A close friend of Bonnard, with whom he is usually 62 connected, he was a very private man, living for much of his life with his mother and choosing his subject matter for the most part from the cameoed details of everyday domestic life, a theme explored extensively by the Japanese.

61 Bonnard *Street Corner*, from *Quelques aspects de la vie de Paris* 1899

62 Vuillard *The Avenue*,
from *Paysages et intérieurs*
1899

If one compares Vuillard's colour lithograph *The Seamstress*
63 (*c.* 1893), an early venture into print-making, with Suzuki Haruno-
64 bu's *Youth playing a Drum* (1768), one finds the same kind of pose, the
same type of patterned background divided by a door, the same
curvilinear flowing drapery, the same colour range of greys, greens
and blues. Vuillard's mother, the model for this work as she was for so
many others, was a seamstress and his uncle, a frequent visitor to their
flat, a textile designer. The influence of Japanese artists such as
Hiroshige, who revelled in the depiction of highly decorated surfaces,
must have combined with these family activities to instil in Vuillard a
constant fascination with highly decorative units within an overall
plain composition. In Hokusai's view of Mount Fuji from the
Gohyaku Rakan-ji temple (which also influenced Monet in his
painting of the terrace at Sainte-Adresse), each of the temple
prostitutes is wearing a kimono, each decorated in a different pattern.
In Vuillard's *Les Tuileries*, a lithograph published in *L'Oeuvre* in 1893,
a group of people with their backs to the spectator, as in the Hokusai
print, are looking out into space and each is clad in a vividly patterned
shawl or dress. Vuillard virtually stopped producing prints after about
1902 but the effect of them on his paintings remained always
perceptible, as he continued to merit Aurier's description of him as 'a
rare colourist, full of charm and improvisation, a poet able to
communicate, not without some irony, the mellow emotions of life,
the tenderness of intimate interiors'.

It is quite likely that the Nabis and other Post-Impressionists
misunderstood the real nature of Japanese art; it is possible too that, as
with the Impressionists, it did no more than fortify their belief in
innovations which they were already discovering themselves, as
Ernest Chesneau had suggested as early as 1878 in an article in the
Gazette des Beaux-Arts: 'Painters found a confirmation rather than an
inspiration for their personal ways of seeing, feeling, understanding
and interpreting nature. The result was a redoubling of individual
originality.' In any case, by the end of the first decade of the twentieth
century overt Japanese influence only lingered in the decorative arts
and the works of minor painters. But its overall impact had been
significant, especially as disseminated through posters, prints and
illustrations. It had confirmed the liberation of colour from a purely
descriptive role and introduced notions of linear simplicity and
boldness of outline which became essential elements in many of the
new styles that were to follow each other in Western art for the next
century. It had proved that *chiaroscuro* was not essential to painting

63 Vuillard *The
Seamstress, c.* 1893

64 Harunobu *Youth
playing a Drum* 1768

65 Gauguin *The Vision after the Sermon: The Struggle of Jacob and the Angel* 1888

66 Van Gogh *The Italian Woman* 1887–8

and that art could progress without the kind of preoccupation with light and shade which had given Impressionism an essential part of its dynamism. It moved European painting perceptibly closer to the possibility of pure abstraction.

In their rummage through the newly fashionable art forms of the past and in their desire to abandon conventional distinctions between 'high' and 'low' art, the Post-Impressionists touched on many sources of possible inspiration including Limoges enamels, twelfth-century stained glass and a host of minor decorative elements. They made constant reference to Egyptian art, which was receiving a good deal of attention from archaeologists and historians – Lucien Pissarro was not 67 the only artist of the time to sit in the Louvre or the British Museum drawing the recently acquired treasures from the land of the Pharaohs. But the word 'Egyptian' was used in a way which was both laudatory and inaccurate to describe works of art which had a hieratic gnomic quality and were not representational in the accepted sense of the word. The images produced by the monks of Beuron (*see* p. 112) – which in fact were loosely Byzantine, if anything – were seen by their makers as conforming to 'Egyptian' canons of beauty, and the Douanier Rousseau described Picasso on one occasion as an 'Egyptian' painter. In one of his possibly fictionalized diatribes recorded by Charles Morice in his book about Gauguin, published in 1920, the artist is reported as saying, 'in a deep and hoarse voice':

Primitive art proceeds from the mind and uses nature. So-called refined art proceeds from sensuality and serves nature. Nature is the servant of the former and the mistress of the latter. But the servant cannot forget her origin and degrades the artist by letting him adore her. This is how we have fallen into the abominable error of naturalism, which began with the Greeks of Pericles. Since then the more or less great artists have been only those who reacted against this error. But their reactions have been only awakenings of memory, gleams of common sense in a movement of decadence which fundamentally has lasted for centuries. Truth is to be found in a purely cerebral art, in a primitive art – the most erudite of all in Egypt. There lies the principle. In our present plight the only possible salvation lies in a reasoned and frank return to principle.

Disregarding the nonsensical element in this *aperçu* of the history of art, the reference to Egypt and to 'primitive art' is significant. A profound change was taking place in the apprehension of the primitive and indeed of the historical evaluation of the development of civilization.

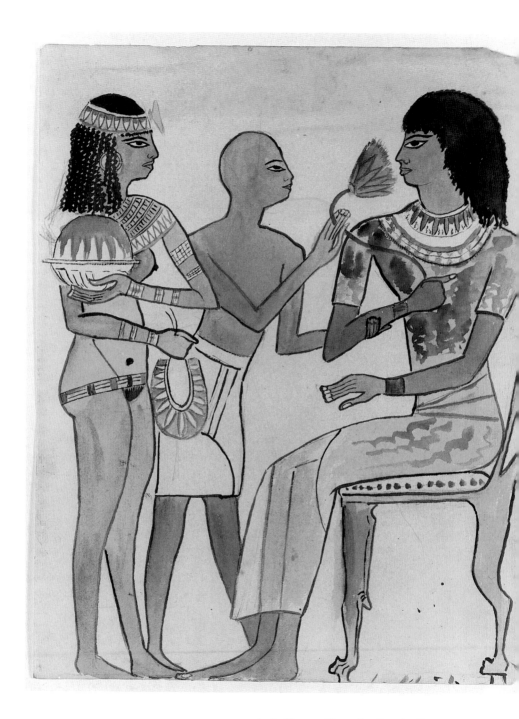

67 L. Pissarro *Copy after Egyptian Fresco, c.* 1880

In the course of the nineteenth century the British, the French, the Germans, the Belgians, the Italians and the Dutch either seized vast overseas possessions or explored and exploited those they already had. No longer content with the generally laissez-faire attitudes which eighteenth-century colonialists had adopted – in most fields save the economic – and fired with a passion for categorization and documentation, European scientists, archaeologists, anthropologists, 68, 69 historians and missionaries descended like a swarm of fact-hungry locusts on lands which previously had been denied the dignity of past histories. Sometimes these activities were not as well-intentioned as their results turned out to be. In 1897, for instance, a British 'punitive' naval expedition sent to the state of Benin plundered the king's palace and brought back to Europe a vast hoard of bronze sculpture which represents one of the finest productions of African tribal art. These

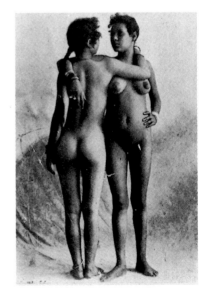

68 Fang mask from Gabon, which belonged to Vlaminck and Derain

69 Magazine photograph used by Matisse for his *Two Negresses* sculpture of 1908

were judiciously distributed amongst British museums, though many remained in the temporary possession of the men who had acquired them; within a decade they were to be found in the museums of Leipzig, Paris, Berlin and Dresden and in the private collections of artists such as Picasso.

In the evolutionist theories which had dominated European thinking since Darwin, 'primitive' art was seen as an inferior cultural phenomenon because it depended too heavily upon the materials of which it was made and failed to come up to the representational capabilities achieved by Europeans. Artistic merit was assessed by its ability to imitate. By the second half of the century, however, as

70 Palais des colonies, 1889 Universal Exhibition, Paris

aesthetics, art history and anthropology became more sophisticated, these certainties began to be eroded. Writers such as William Morris, defending the nature of medieval art, advocated a return to primitive craftsmanship. In Vienna the art historian Alois Riegl was propounding in the 1890s the theory that imitation was an entirely alien concept to 'barbaric' artists and that the most important thing about a work of art was its 'visibility', its expressiveness, not its relationship to external objects or beliefs. This viewpoint became all the more persuasive as the mid-century tenets began to waver. The simplicities of Newtonian physics were being undermined by Einstein and others, the certainties of human choice were being questioned by psychologists such as Freud and the materialist historic determinism of Marx limited Romantic notions about the nature of individual creativity. Never again would people be able to look upon visual reality and its imitation as necessarily integral to art.

The Impressionists' promotion of the idea of an optical scientific vision different from the conceptual had opened up all kinds of avenues of exploration. The Japanese had shown how line could be liberated from volume and colour over flat areas used to express emotion and feeling. Now the primitive art of 'colonial' peoples 80 demonstrated that there were viable alternatives to the rational perspectival conventions of post-Renaissance art and that they were endowed furthermore with that kind of innocence associated with the Garden of Eden which had intermittently beguiled Europeans since the time of Rousseau. Even from the purely stylistic point of view there was the fact that most primitive art was geometric, which commended it to those who sought to replace the looseness of Impressionism with a formal structuralism of the kind variously pioneered by Cézanne and Seurat. Moreover, knowledge of these primitive art forms was not merely notional. The great 1889 Paris 70 exhibition displayed a Buddhist temple, a Moroccan bazaar, a Chinese pavilion, a reconstructed Cairo street, a Senegalese village, a Vietnamese theatrical troupe and a Javanese *kampong*. It was in the latter that Debussy first heard Gamelan music, which he said made Palestrina's counterpoint sound like child's play. Edmond de Goncourt recorded in his *Journal* some time later the reactions of Rodin:

While we were walking before dinner, Rodin spoke to me about his admiration for the Javanese dancers and of the sketches he made of them, 71, 72 quick sketches which did not adequately convey their exoticism. He also talked about similar studies of a Japanese village transplanted to London, where there were also Japanese dancers.

71 Rodin *Drawing of a Cambodian Dancer* 1906

72 Rodin drawing a Cambodian dancer, from *L'Illustration* 1906

Nobody typified the nostalgia for the symbol-laden creeds of the primitive and the non-European or publicized them more extensively than Gauguin. Primitive art made its appearance at a very early stage in his life, fostered in the first instance no doubt by the influence of his maternal grandmother, the illegitimate daughter of a poor French-woman and an aristocratic Peruvian Spaniard, a woman intensely proud of her Inca inheritance. When he was 36 and living unhappily and reluctantly in Copenhagen with his wife Mette, he carved for her a most extraordinary wooden jewel box. It was based on a Bronze Age coffin of the kind which Danish archaeologists had been unearthing over the past few decades, with the recumbent figure of a dead youth occupying the role normally played by a mummy. The outside of the box is decorated with bas-relief engravings of ballet dancers *à la* Degas and with Oriental masks, which also appear around

94

the flower-shaped hinges, along with *netsuke* figures. On the lid are two dancing girls, an old woman with rounded breasts, the head of a bulbous-nosed old man and a number of pumpkin-like objects which have been described as schematized skulls.

The whole box is in effect a paradigm of the exotic influences at work on the liberated imaginations of the Post-Impressionists: primitivism, the art of the Orient – and that not only because of the Japanese elements – the old woman with the putative heads has been seen as a reference to Kali, the Hindu goddess of destruction usually depicted with a necklace of skulls – the heritage of Impressionism reflected in the quotations from Degas and the overall effect of an ill-defined symbolism. To read this is, as always in such an area of human expression, not easy. One way is to relate it to the personality of the artist, as Wayne Anderson did in *Gauguin's Paradise Lost* of 1971:

Themes that link death and vanity have long traditions in Western art, dating back to the Middle Ages. Persistently popular among academic painters of the nineteenth century and also strikingly resurgent in *art nouveau*, such themes seem to be fundamental elements of the male psyche. Objects of female vanity are lures, and to be lured is to risk capture and death. Gauguin created the jewel box as a vessel of vanity, both in its function as a container of decorative items and in its motifs, which center around the theme of theatrical life. In this context the jewel box became a coffin, suggesting that female vanity is the cause of man's ultimate death. Like Pandora's box, the age-old symbol of female genitalia, Gauguin's vanity coffin contains the worldly evils.

In creating this morbid gift for his wife, Gauguin was no doubt acting out his bitterness toward her and toward women in general. Yet the motifs juxtaposed on the jewel box are oddly ambiguous, as if his condemnation of female vanity was also a warning of the dangers of licentiousness. The woman with the raised hands is blocking the young girls from woman's fate – in the shape of the lusting, leering old man and the matronly figure with gross breasts . . . In this way Gauguin evoked an idea that was to become an essential theme in his whole symbolic imagery: the wages of sin is ageing and death.

Despite this initial foray into the tangle of primitivism and half-comprehensible imagery, Gauguin's most influential contact at this time with a culture other than that of contemporary France came from closer to home. Steeped in the most rigid traditions of Celtic Catholicism, a royalist enclave in a republican country, Brittany occupied in the French imagination the same role which in Britain was allotted to the Highlands of Scotland. Recently made more accessible to the public by the opening up of the railways, it had started to become a magnet for artists in the late 1870s (Cornwall was undergoing a similar experience at about the same time). In June 1886 Gauguin decided to spend the summer at Pont-Aven, a small village near the south coast of Brittany, some five kilometres from the sea, with a port for sea-going ships. Picturesquely and unselfconsciously clad in traditional costume, its inhabitants combined religiosity, superstition and a contempt for city dwellers in proportions which made them irresistible to the generation of Post-Impressionism. Gauguin spent several months there each year from 1888 to 1891 and in 1894 and 1895. He became the central figure of a whole group of artists, including Bernard, Sérusier, Denis, Jacob Meyer de Haan, Jan Verkade, Charles Filiger and O'Connor, that came to be known as the School of Pont-Aven and formed the nucleus of the Café Volpini exhibitions. They practised a style they called Synthetism, which stressed the abstract qualities of line, colour and form, drew heavily upon medieval and early Renaissance art, looked for inspiration to Puvis de Chavannes and eschewed the use of contemporary colours. But in fact it never quite achieved that emancipation from subject matter which it promised and Denis's famous aphorism ('Remember that before it is a charger, a nude, or an anecdote, a painting is essentially a flat surface covered with colours in a certain order') was not fully translated into pictorial reality until the opening decades of the next century.

By and large the Pont-Aven School (the phrase had become current by 1890) was known and recognized not so much for its style as its subject matter, with Breton peasant women abounding, a vague air of mystical piety (*see* Chapter 4) and a diffused symbolism that found its most cogent expression in Gauguin's *Vision after the Sermon*   65 (1888). Simple shapes derived from pious imagery and woodcuts, flat areas of Japanese-inspired colour, figures quoted from a print by Hokusai are all blended to create an icon of primitive belief. The theme of the painting is that, after a Sunday sermon, the pious Breton women have a vision of the subject which the priest had taken for his text. Such a notion would not have been found bizarre by a generation that happily accepted the apparition of the Virgin Mary to a peasant girl at Lourdes and saw nothing unusual in similar visits by divine persons to a Carmelite nun resident in Lisieux. In a letter to van Gogh, however, Gauguin hedged his bets:

I believe that in these figures I have achieved a great rustic and *superstitious* simplicity. To me in this painting the landscape and the struggle exist only in the imagination of these praying people as a result of the sermon. That is why there is a contrast between these real people and the struggle which takes place in a landscape which is not real, and is out of all proportion.

Back in Paris after painting *Vision after the Sermon*, he found the Universal Exhibition a source of excitement and inspiration. He visited it several times and was especially impressed by the leaflets designed to attract French people to emigrate, which recounted the charms of life in colonies such as Tahiti. When he returned to Brittany it was with an enhanced respect for primitive art and a yearning for the simple life of 'uncivilized' people. In the meantime he turned more enthusiastically than before to the examples of a primitive style   73 which he found around him, basing his *Yellow Christ* on a crucifix in   74 the twelfth-century chapel of Trémalo near Pont-Aven and his *Green Christ* on the Calvary group in the village of Nizon.

73 A Breton calvary, Menhir de Pleuven

77 Cézanne *The Murderer* 1867

stencilled lettering, which is very similar to the Douanier Rousseau's portrait of Joseph Brummer.

The most spectacular sign of a new understanding of primitive art was indeed in the emergence of the Douanier Rousseau, the earliest of whose works had appeared in 1877 and the first of whose paintings was exhibited in 1883. Although they provoked conventional derision, he became a member of the Indépendants and between 1886 and 1902 exhibited regularly some five and ten paintings each year. Redon was one of the first to praise his works, Camille Pissarro found them admirable, stating that with him 'emotion takes the place of training', and in 1891 Vallotton described one of Rousseau's tigers as 'the alpha and omega of art'.

79 Rousseau *Myself: Landscape Portrait* 1890

78 Cézanne *Portrait of Achille Emperaire, c.* 1868–70

81 Ranson *Christ and Buddha* 1895

CHAPTER FOUR

A Thirst for Commitment

The Impressionists had deprived themselves of a whole range of inspirational stimuli that in the past had provided a vocabulary of imagery at once emotive and immediately comprehensible. Concerned almost exclusively with the depiction of contemporary life and with the appeal of nature and its transient effects, they had gone far in elevating paintings into objects independent of any extraneous effects, such as religious or political emotions, other than those which could be directly perceived by the eye. They discarded classical iconography with all its literary and academic resonances. Not for them scenes of historic interest, nor those likely to stir sentiments of patriotic fervour. Manet painted a few religious subjects, more as a gesture towards the Old Masters and as a step towards his own official recognition than as exercises in visual piety, but no Impressionist ever ventured on a Madonna or portrayed Joan of Arc. The patriotic themes which stirred a Meissonier or the political fervour which 83 prompted Delacroix to paint *Liberty leading the People* had no appeal to painters such as Renoir or Monet, any more than they had to writers such as Flaubert, the Goncourts or Zola. But such ideological abnegation was not easy to support. A passion for belief can be a great, if sometimes fatal, incentive to creativity. Moreover, between 1870 and 1890 the tides of conviction in France had altered considerably. The humiliation imposed by the Franco-Prussian war (1870–71), the hatreds, resentments and fear stimulated by the Commune (1871) and its suppression, with the massacre of priests and workers, had exacerbated divisions which had existed since the seventeenth century between rationalists and believers, between the upholders of the old order and the protagonists of the new. Nor were these divisions in any way lessened by the reverberations of the Dreyfus case (1897–9).

At first it had seemed as though the schism which rent France was a straightforward one with all the intelligence, tolerance and originality on one side and reactionary conservatism and anti-intellectualism on the other. In fact that had never quite been the case, as the examples of Chateaubriand, Montalembert and Lamartine suggest, but after 1870

the position had become far more complex. A growing discontent
82 with the all too apparent evils of consumer capitalism produced
reactions other than the purely political and it was accompanied by a
Catholic revival, almost as potent as the Counter-Reformation,
which found its expression in the Vatican Council of 1870 and the
proclamation of papal infallibility. Taking place in most European
countries, this reaction was especially powerful in France where a
spate of new cults devoted to saintly figures, tailored to meet the needs
of the time – the Curé d'Ars, Bernadette of Lourdes, Theresa of
Lisieux and eventually Joan of Arc – stimulated the piety of the
masses, whilst the newly invented cult of the Sacred Heart reached
almost epidemic proportions, finding expression in the esoteric
architectural fantasy of the basilica of the Sacré-Coeur on Montmartre, the religious response to the secular, scientific and rational
totem of the Eiffel Tower.

The appeal of this renascent Catholicism was not merely to
84, 88 the masses. It had assumed cultural and intellectual dimensions. It is

82 Herkomer *Hard Times* 1885

83 Meissonier *The Barricades: Rue de la Mortellerie, June 1848*

significant that whereas in 1848 there were only some 3000 monks in France, by 1901 the number had risen to 37,000. Whilst the so-called secular clergy, who worked in parishes, were largely drawn from the peasant and working classes, monastic orders demanded a higher degree of intellectual ability and monasteries often became centres of cultural activity. At the Benedictine abbey of Solesmes, for instance, there took place a remarkable revival of plainsong, based on the most exhaustive historical research, which had a profound effect on the work of composers such as César Franck. In the visual arts the most significant achievement took place outside France at the abbey of Beuron in Hohenzollern, where in the 1890s the monks evolved a unique, hieratic art form (with strong Egyptian undercurrents) that rejected Renaissance notions of perspective and relied upon a canon of human forms ultimately of divine origin – a useful stimulus to desultory creative impulses. One of Gauguin's followers, Jan Verkade, who had been converted to Catholicism, became a monk there in 1894. Denis and Sérusier visited the abbey and kept up a revealing correspondence with him for several years.

93

84 Osbert *The Vision*
(St Genevieve) 1892

85 Moreau *Young Girl carrying the Head of Orpheus* 1865

87 Sérusier *Tobias and the Angel, c.* 1895

86 Moreau *Mystic Flower, c.* 1890

In many cases, as with Verkade and the Jewish artist Mögens Ballin, a conversion to Catholicism took place as a kind of personal revelation of almost Pauline intensity. This is exemplified in the case of the novelist and influential art critic Joris-Karl Huysmans, who played a significant role in the Post-Impressionist period. After writing novels such as *À Rebours* (1884) which hymned the praises of sensuousness and the importance of cultivated self-indulgence, he took to religion in a big way and became an oblate in a Benedictine monastery. More academic painters such as James Tissot and Gustave Doré, perhaps with the incentive of intimations of mortality, forsook the depiction of the pains and pleasures of contemporary life for Biblical scenes, episodes from the life of Christ. Puvis de Chavannes's forays into religious imagery, especially his *History of Sainte Geneviève* (1874–8) which adorned the walls of the Panthéon, excited the admiration of Gauguin and Seurat as well as of the general public. Gustave Moreau,

85 whose works served as such potent incentives to the Symbolists, relied heavily on religious imagery for his mysteriously evocative paintings. Gauguin's admiration of them was qualified only by the proviso that

103 they were too 'literary' and, though Moreau's versions of the Salome story have dimensions other than the literary, paintings such as *The*

86 *Mystic Flower*, with its near metamorphosis of the Virgin Mary and its pyramid of adoring saints all set in a bizarre landscape, typify the allusive metaphors which became an integral part of one aspect of late nineteenth-century art.

The attractions of Catholicism were unexpectedly experienced by the young. Later in life Bernard described the change which came over him at the age of 24:

I became a Catholic, ready to fight for the church, the upholder of all traditions and the generous symbol of the most noble sentiments. I became intoxicated with incense, with organ music, prayers, and I returned to the past isolating myself more and more from my own period whose preoccupations with industrialism disgusted me.

Until this point Bernard's work had shown a great vitality and versatility, including in its subject matter brothel scenes as well as paintings and prints of contemporary Breton life, all of them marked by flattened figures, interesting lighting effects and experimentation with the medium. These qualities were particularly noticeable in his

91 zincographs and in the woodcuts of around 1891 which reveal more clearly even than Gauguin's the influence of popular images of the *images d'Epinal* type and the chap-books of the late sixteenth and early

91 Bernard *Bretonneries*,
zincograph cover of
album, 1889

seventeenth centuries. His conversion to religious art, however, put
an end to this florescence of talent and his religious paintings are
marked by a certain shallow decorative quality. At the same time he
retained a keen and perceptive critical sense and remained through his
writings – especially on Gauguin and Cézanne – an important figure
in the development of avant-garde painting.

Bernard attributed his religious interests to his stay at Pont-Aven,
and Brittany was an ideal nursery for the development of cultural
nostalgia. This was especially evident in the work of Paul Sérusier,
who spent most of his life there, first at Pont-Aven and Le Pouldu,
then at Châteauneuf-du-Faou. Moving stylistically from a straight-

92 Puvis de Chavannes *The Dream* 1883

forward academic style to a version of Gauguin's Synthetism, he produced in 1888 a painting, *The Talisman*, which was seen by Denis 130 as 'a passionate equivalent of an experienced sensation'. It was this work that was mainly responsible for the foundation of the Nabis, a group of painters including Ranson, Denis, Bonnard, Vuillard, Roussel and Ibels who sought to transform painting in terms of the principles and techniques demonstrated in *The Talisman* and who had been fellow pupils of Sérusier both at the Lycée Condorcet and the Académie Julian. Their name, derived from the Hebrew *neebin* meaning 'prophets', had been suggested to them by a Hebrew scholar Auguste Cazalis. Holding regular meetings at the studio of Paul Ranson, an artist of wide erudition who later founded an art school of 81 considerable importance, they discussed art, religion and theosophy – then very fashionable in France – evolved a style of painting marked by an emotional and expressive use of colour and, having held one exhibition at Durand-Ruel's in 1899, drifted apart. Sérusier continued to maintain a strong interest in religion as a stimulus to art and in 93 his increasing concern with creating a mathematical formula of painting drew close to the aesthetic dogmatism of Beuron. Another potent influence on him was the Petit Théâtre des Marionettes, founded in 1888, which was seen as the epitome of Symbolist imagery, and the similar private puppet theatres run by Ranson and Bonnard's brother-in-law. Many of Sérusier's works, such as *Tobias* 87 *and the Angel*, show the formalized gestures, the flat silhouette-like figures and the emphatic decorative backgrounds (designed by artists such as Maillol) which characterized the productions of the Petit Théâtre, where the themes were often drawn from the Old Testament or Classical mythology.

Sérusier was intimate with Denis, who was even more closely identified with the Catholic revival. His first spectacular success was a painting exhibited at the Salon des Indépendants in 1891, entitled *Catholic Mystery*, which was also inscribed with the Greek word 89 'Aspasmos', the equivalent of 'Hail', implying the salutation of the angel Gabriel to the Virgin Mary. The angel, however, has assumed the guise of a priest with an open missal, preceded by two altar boys with candles, thus emphasizing the continuing role of the church mediating between God and man. Although the work is painted in Pointillist dots, applied to flat layers of colour, the total effect is decorative rather than constructive, and the setting of the scene in what is clearly a modern room is an exploitation of an idea of transferring the religious past into the present. This had first become

financed by de la Rochefoucauld, who was to be his most supportive
90   patron. Typical of these is his *Virgin and Child* with its Breton
background, its emaciated Christchild and its Cimabuesque faces. He
was preoccupied with mystical concerns, mostly Christian but mixed
with theosophical and other strains.

   Much of Gauguin's imagery is shot through with religious
references, though often of a slightly profane kind. The implications
74   are diverse. In the Breton pictures he identifies himself with Christ, a
notion which kept reappearing in his thinking as he sought for
symbols to bolster the image of himself and that justification of his
artistic personality after which he so patently hungered. In his
Tahitian works he reverted time and time again to motifs of Christian
iconography – the birth of Christ, angels, Adam and Eve, Paradise
94   and of course the Virgin Mary. The difference between Gauguin and
most of the other artists who became concerned with religion is that,
whereas they looked upon it as a guide and discipline which would
supply them with the artistic certainties they craved, he ravaged its
imagery and exploited its psychological resonances in the pursuit of
his own overpowering creative passions.

   Secular ideologies, however, also began to play a role which they
had never played before. On the whole the Impressionists had few
political convictions and certainly hardly ever allowed any they may
have had to be expressed in their art. Renoir, Cézanne and Degas had
been more or less straightforward reactionaries, stoutly anti-Dreyfus
and deploring the spread of education amongst the working classes.
Manet was critical of the establishment, except when it suited him not
to be, and accepted membership of the Légion d'Honneur with a
pleasure only modified by the fact that it was so late in arriving. On
the other hand, he did do a number of drawings and lithographs
during the suppression of the Commune of a Daumier-like quality
suggestive of sympathy with the rebels.

   The only real exception was Camille Pissarro, always, as it were, a
crypto-Post-Impressionist, whose sympathies were consistently with
the left and who allowed them to influence his work. Actuated by a
desire to depict the life of the peasantry, he lived almost continuously
in rustic communities such as those at Louveciennes, Pontoise and
Eragny and produced a large number of paintings, drawings and
prints featuring not only work in the fields but market days and other
communal activities. Less authentic and emotive than van Gogh's
peasant images, they were viewed, as he himself admitted in a letter to
Lucien, from the position of an outsider:

124

94 Gauguin *Hail Mary*, woodcut in *Noa Noa* 1893

The man who most completely identified art with anarchism was
the redoubtable Félix Fénéon, who may well be thought of as the
most important influence on practically every manifestation of Post-
Impressionism. An early and enthusiastic supporter of Seurat, whose
scientific approach to art he saw as part of his own concern with
enlarging the potential creativity of ordinary people, his first
significant work had been *Les Impressionnistes en 1886*, a pamphlet
written in his own idiosyncratic style. In it he had invented the word
Neo-Impressionism, which he saw as a movement providing
Impressionism with the scientific structuralism and seriousness it
lacked, describing splendidly the imagery which the older painters
had favoured:

Flowering gardens of Vétheuil, blazing chequerboards of tulips in Holland,
haggard apparitions of locomotives leaving the station, spangled camouf-
lages of Paris on Bastille Day, ice floes on the Seine, magical configurations of
Antibes, amethyst hills, parasol pines and olive trees, the Norman coast, the
Breton coast – such a variety of paintings is determined by geography and
the seasons. Nowhere is the real essence, the quiddity of a scene surveyed and
plotted in an unexpected or emotional manner, everywhere evident the self-
indulgence of a painter using his colours to transfer nature to the canvas.

97 Vallotton *Fénéon in the Office of La Revue Blanche* 1896

Fénéon was insistent too that the artist should pursue a more rigorous
quest for a realism which would be socially observant and not just   98, 99
pleasingly observational. He was especially attracted to the work of
Luce. Unlike Fénéon who was a fairly high-ranking civil servant or
Signac and Seurat who were both well-to-do, Luce was a member of
the working class and always retained its habits and attitudes. In a
review published in 1891 Fénéon described Luce and his work:

He's a newcomer, a tough, loyal fellow with a primitive, muscular talent. In
garrets ungraced by women, a bare-chested worker scrubs himself, another   100
dunks his crust of bread in a bowl. He chooses to paint scenes of the
dilapidated areas of Paris around the fortifications.

Luce had been converted to political radicalism when aged 13 he
had seen bunches of Communards being shot out of hand by
government troops. His sense of commitment was much deeper than
that of most other artists. This became evident in 1894 when Fénéon
was arrested on charges of being in possession of explosives and a few
weeks later was joined by Luce, who was accused of painting pictures
of workers and distributing lithographs of them. 'The arrest of Luce',
reported an anonymous police spy, 'has planted terror in the hearts of
all the illustrators, sculptors and painters of Montmartre; even the
most moderate of anarchists talk of fleeing.' After some months in the
Mazas prison in the place de la Bastille, where Luce drew two pictures
of him subsequently converted into lithographs, Fénéon along with
twenty-nine other anarchists came to trial and, after a brilliantly witty
verbal duel with the judge, he and the rest were acquitted.

The trial had two effects. Unexpectedly it marked the end of
anarchist violence in France but, on the other hand, it evoked a
remarkable display of artistic solidarity. Fénéon was defended in the
papers by famous writers such as Arsène Alexandre, Gustave Kahn,
Octave Mirbeau and Louise Michel. Mallarmé spoke in his defence at
the trial, Verlaine denied that he could have any contact with
anarchists. His lawyer was Edgar Demange, a friend of Thadée
Natanson, the owner and editor of La Révue Blanche and himself a
lawyer who helped in the defence. Later in 1894 Demange was also to
defend Dreyfus in the celebrated case which prompted Forain and
Caran d'Ache to start a memorably satirical and anti-Dreyfus four-
page caricature weekly Psst!.

The police spy's reference to Montmartre was interesting because
in no other part of Paris were art and radical politics so intermingled as
in that faubourg, where the Commune had started in 1871.

98 Morbelli *For 80 Cents* 1895

99 Cormon *The Forge* 1893

100 Luce *Workman washing Himself* 1886–7

the Neo-Impressionists, the Nabis and Toulouse-Lautrec, he wrote *inter alia*:

When you visit this place, comrades, don't just eye the pictures, get a load of the mugs of the posh. There's no denying it, what that lot knows about anything that's new and spunky isn't worth a fart. Some hee-haw like donkeys, others beef away, and those who do like to air their views sound like piss-pots under a sick man's arse . . . One who has a hell of a nerve is Toulouse. Nothing stuck up about *his* colour or drawing. Some white, some black, some red in bloody big splashes and simple forms; that's his scene. And there's nobody to touch him in painting the mugs of drivelling money-bags boozing away with street-wise tarts slobbering over them for a bit of lolly.

He then went on to advocate ideas already familiar in England but only gaining familiarity in France through the activities of some of the Post-Impressionists:

With any luck, damn it, the day will come when art will become part of the life of every Tom, Dick and Harry, just like chops and beer. When that happens everything, plates, spoons, chairs, beds, every bloody thing will have smart lines and smashing colours. When that happens the so-called 'artist' will stop looking down his nose at the worker. They'll both be brothers.

The most startling expression of this spirit had been the creation in 1882 by the writer Jules Lévy of 'Les Incohérents', a group of writers and artists united in their desire to question conventions, distrust the rational and canonize the absurd, the direct forerunners in effect of both the Dadaists and the Surrealists. From 1882 onwards the Incohérents held a series of annual exhibitions (they were appropriately replaced by an annual ball) which attracted a great deal of publicity, almost all hostile. These included works such as a rectangular board painted white by Alphonse Allais entitled *First Communion of Anaemic Young Girls in the Snow*, a cardboard sun rising out of a bidet, a bearded female nude entitled *Monsieur Vénus de Milo*, a painting of a baby 'not knowing which breast to suckle'. Toulouse-Lautrec exhibited regularly, his contributions including 'Soda-water-colours', a work painted on sandpaper entitled *The Batignolles $3\frac{1}{2}BC$* and sculpture made of bread. A common feature of all the exhibitions was the parodying of works of art by painters of repute such as Puvis de Chavannes.

The Post-Impressionists exemplified a link between art and various ideologies closer than had ever consciously existed before and which persisted almost the whole of the twentieth century, manifesting itself in such various forms as Social Realism – the totalitarian aesthetic

doctrines of Germany and the USSR – and the spate of art prompted
by such events as the Spanish Civil War, the Atom Bomb and the
Vietnam War. In the 1930s, for instance, when Signac was writing
introductions to exhibitions of Communist paintings in France,
Picasso was painting *Guernica*, Léger was creating his powerful
iconography of working-class life, Grosz was excoriating the Nazis
and the Surrealists were imposing a rigid Communist orthodoxy on
their members. Whether these activities had any actual influence on
events is doubtful but beside the point. The Post-Impressionists had
been the first to show that when art was bereft of a central orthodoxy,
driven by its own impetus to react positively against the imposition of
a stylistic uniformity and riven by artistic sectarianism, it was at least
desirable to have some notional framework. Even when this did not
involve religious or political elements, it involved some form of
aesthetic belief. Never before had artists felt so impelled to join
groups, to issue manifestos. If the battle between the avant-garde and
the establishment can be likened to a cowboys and Indians situation, it
had become apparent that the Indians were strictly tribal.

102 Toulouse-Lautrec *Le Dernier Salut*,
cover for *Le Mirliton*, March 1887

103 Moreau *The Apparition* 1874–6

105 Bonnard, cover of *La Revue Blanche* 1894

largely fictionalized conversations with him, first published in the *Mercure de France* and then in book form (*Souvenirs sur Paul Cézanne*, 1912), helped to establish the position of that artist as an innovator whose work had presaged the future developments of painting.

Bernard had commenced the most creative period of his career as a disciple of Gauguin at Pont-Aven and had done much to publicize his works, but broke violently with him as a result of an article by Aurier, entitled 'Symbolisme en peinture: Paul Gauguin', which appeared in the *Mercure de France* in March 1891. It made no reference at all to Bernard, who saw himself as the main originator of the kind of painting about which Aurier was writing. Aurier himself was a young Symbolist poet, who had already written eloquently about van Gogh. The application of the word to painting was an indication not only of the extent to which, since Impressionism, artists and critics were anxious to fit art into categories of belief but also of an entirely new and intimate relationship between literature and painting. In literature it had made its first formal appearance in 1886 in an article by Moréas, who underlined the reactions against both purely aesthetic ideas of 'art for art's sake' and the often naive positivism of Realism in favour of using words which by their sound and symbolism would suggest states of mind and convey subtleties of feeling.

After condemning Impressionism as 'a faithful translation of an exclusively sensory impression, without going further', Aurier went on to define the purpose and nature of the new art:

The normal and final goal of painting, as of all the arts, cannot be a direct presentation of objects. Its ultimate aim is to express Ideas by translating them into a special language. To the eyes of the artist objects are meaningless as objects. They can only appear to him as *signs*. The artist has an obligation to avoid that antithesis of all art: concrete truth, illusionism, *trompe l'oeil*, so as not to give by his pictures that false impression of nature which would act on the spectator just as nature itself. The strict duty of the ideological painter is therefore to make a rational choice among the multiple elements which exist in objective reality, and to use in his work only the general and individual lines, forms and colours which serve to express the ideological significance of the general symbol. The artist will also have the right – an obvious deduction – to exaggerate, to attenuate, to deform those directly significant elements of form, line and colour, not only according to his individual vision, but also to make any deformations needed to express the Idea.

Thus to sum up, the work of art, as I have chosen to evoke it logically will be:

1. *Ideological*, because its sole ideal is the expression of the Idea.
2. *Symbolist*, because it expresses the Idea through forms.

106
107

106 Cross *Nocturne* 1896

107 Roussel *Composition: Women in the Forest* 1890–92

145

3. *Synthetic*, because it presents these forms, these signs in such a way that they can be generally understood.
4. *Subjective*, because the object presented is considered not merely as an object, but as the sign of an idea suggested by the subject.
5. (And therefore) *Decorative*, since truly decorative painting as conceived by the Egyptians and probably by the Greeks and the primitives, is nothing but a manifestation of art which is at the same time subjective and synthetic.

Couched in the language of the 1890s, proliferating with capitals, and later containing sentences such as 'Oh! how rare are those whose bodies and hearts are moved by the sublime spectacle of pure Being and our Ideas', Aurier's statement, though tailored to the specific need of exalting Gauguin, could be seen as a charter for most avant-garde movements of the next century. It proved how far the reaction against the work of art as a representation of reality, which was to be judged by how far it had captured that reality, had gone.

Although Aurier's statement was one of the most explicit affirmations of this new attitude, it was not the only one. Charles Henry, poet, philosopher and scientist, who moved in the same artistic circles, had published a widely read book on the psychological and emotional attributes of objects and Aurier had picked up many ideas from the writers who had already called themselves Symbolists.

108 Interviewed in the *Écho de Paris* in March 1891, Mallarmé said:

In a society without stability, without unity, no stable or definitive art can be created. This unfinished social organization which explains at the same time the restlessness of all minds gives birth to the unexplained need for individuality of which the present literary manifestations are a direct reflection.

He then went on to describe the essence of these literary manifestations in words which *mutatis mutandis* echo Aurier's about painting:

To *name* an object is to suppress three quarters of the enjoyment of the poem which consists of the pleasure of apprehending little by little; to *suggest* it that is the dream. It is the perfect utilization of this mystery that constitutes symbolism to evoke an object bit by bit in order to show a mood, or conversely to choose an object and extract a mood from it by a series of deciphering.

Mallarmé was in effect a significant figure in the transition from Impressionism. He had been a close friend of Manet, who painted a memorable portrait of him and illustrated his translation of Poe's *The Raven*. He himself was a talented draughtsman who illustrated many of his letters with charming sketches. He was on close terms with

108 Gauguin *Portrait of Stéphane Mallarmé* 1891

Whistler, Munch, Redon, Renoir – who did a drawing for a projected book of his verse – Gauguin and many others. The Tuesday night parties in his flat in the rue de Rome became the centre of the whole Symbolist movement, gathering together both writers and painters. Of the many shared interests between the two, a typical one was the book on the solar origins of mythology by the English writer G. W. Cox, which Mallarmé translated as *Les Dieux antiques* and which was used as an inspiration for some of the imagery of both Moreau and Redon.

109

Moreau, although he was in his 60s by the time that Symbolism had really seized the minds and imaginations of poets and painters, was a key figure in the evolution of the Symbolist elements in the reactions against Impressionism. He created a world of exotic fantasies, luxurious sensationalism, mystically erotic, hinting at sensual depravities existing under a veneer of religious iconography. These qualities were not so much the products of an unconscious urge as the expression of powerful emotions about which he wrote with vehement feeling:

103

Oh noble poetry of living and impassioned silence! How admirable is that art which under a material guise is a mirror of physical beauty, reflecting the movements of the soul, of the spirit, of the heart and the imagination; which responds to those divine necessities felt by humanity throughout the ages. It is the language of God! To this eloquence, whose character, nature and power have until now resisted definition, I have given all my solicitude, all my efforts; the evocation of thought through line, arabesque and all the devices available to the plastic arts – that has been my aim.

His efforts brought him widespread recognition: from the establishment which bestowed on him the Officer Class of the Légion d'Honneur, membership of the Institut and a teaching professorship at the École des Beaux-Arts; from the literary and artistic opposition in the shape of that most sincere form of flattery, imitation. Mallarmé was inspired by his works and so too, above all others, was one of the most representative figures of fin-de-siècle France, Joris-Karl Huysmans. Always drawn to the visual arts and a critic of force and distinction, Huysmans had initially been influenced by Degas's paintings of the ballet, the circus and the brothel. In his *Croquis Parisiens* of 1880, for instance, his description of an acrobatic performance at the Folies Bergère is an almost exact verbal transcript of Degas's painting of Miss La La at the Cirque Fernando; in his novel *Marthe* (1876) he relied heavily on Degas's monotypes of *maisons*

109 Redon, 1889 illustration for Flaubert's *La Tentation de Saint Antoine*

closes. But at the Salon of 1880 he was smitten by Moreau and wrote enthusiastically about him in *L'Art Moderne* as

a mystic shut up in the heart of Paris in a cell which is not even reached by the noise of contemporary life, though it furiously beats against the doors of his cloister. Plunged in ecstasy, he sees the radiance of fairy-like visions, apotheosis of other ages . . . After having been haunted by Mantegna and by Leonardo, whose princesses move through mysterious landscapes of black and blue, M. Moreau has been seized by an enthusiasm for the hieratic arts of India, and from the two currents of Italian and Hindu art he has, spurred forward also by the feverish colours of Delacroix, developed an art which is peculiarly his own, an art which is personal and new, whose disquieting flavour is at first disconcerting.

The number of people who read *L'Art Moderne* must have been relatively small compared with those who read Huysmans's sensational novel *À Rebours* published four years later, which became a bible of what might be called symbolic decadence. In it the hero Des Esseintes lauds Moreau at great length and describes his paintings, one of which he possesses, as 'disquieting and sinister allegories' created by an artist 'haunted by the symbols of superhuman perversities and superhuman loves'.

Des Esseintes was largely based on Comte Robert de Montesquiou, the model for Proust's Baron de Charlus and a great devotee of Moreau. Proust himself had first seen Moreau's works in the salon of Madame Straus, the mother of one of his school friends, and, fired by Montesquiou's enthusiasm, he wrote several articles about the painter which were published together under the title *Notes sur le monde mystérieux de Gustave Moreau* (1898). There are frequent flattering references to Moreau scattered through the pages of *À la recherche du temps perdu*, in which a painting by him hangs on the wall of the hero's room. Moreau's standing with writers was quite remarkable: poets such as Jules Laforgue, one of the pioneers of free verse, novelists such as Pierre Louÿs and Paul Bourget, even musicians such as Debussy, who claimed that his two favourite painters were Botticelli and Moreau, succumbed to the charms they saw in his work. The links between art and literature had never been so intimate as those displayed in the cult of a painter who theoretically presided over a whole strand of Post-Impressionism and influenced artists as disparate as Gauguin and Rouault. When he came to publish *Notes d'un peintre* in 1908, one of Moreau's pupils, Henri Matisse, was still expressing opinions which might have been those of his master:

110 Redon, 'Perhaps nature first tried eyes on flowers', no. 2 from *Les Origines* 1883

Composition is the art of arranging decoratively the various elements which the artist uses to express his feelings . . . There are two ways of expressing things: one is to show them plainly, the other is to evoke them with art. In departing from the *literal* representation of movement, one attains more beauty and grandeur . . . The choice of colours does not depend on any scientific theory; it is based on observation, on feeling, on the dictates of one's own sensibility.

Fourteen years younger than Moreau, Odilon Redon had been untouched by any of the movements which had beguiled his contemporaries and was over 40 when he held his first exhibition in 1881 at the galleries of *La Vie Moderne*. Welcomed enthusiastically by Huysmans, who later became a close friend, he unexpectedly featured in the 1886 Impressionist exhibition. He then started to exhibit at the Indépendants, which he helped to found. When he extended his art from the limitations of black chalk, to which he had previously confined it, and started to use colour, his reputation amongst younger artists increased perceptibly. Gauguin became a fervent admirer and became interested in Madagascar through Redon's wife, who had been born there. It was from one of Redon's illustrations in an album entitled *Origines* of 1883, which showed a drawing of a flower with an eye at its centre, inscribed 'Perhaps nature first tried eyes on flowers', that Gauguin derived the notion of the eye within a flower, a symbol which he used on several occasions. Redon attended the famous farewell banquet to Gauguin on his departure for Tahiti in 1891 and in Gauguin's baggage when he left was a copy of Redon's lithograph *Death*, from which he derived the hooded head that appears in the 1897 woodcut *Be in love, you will be happy*. When he read Huysmans's article about Redon in 1889, which had been titled 'Le Monstre', Gauguin wrote:

I do not see how Odilon Redon makes monsters . . . He is a dreamer, a visionary . . . Nature has mysterious infinities, a power of imagination, it manifests these by always changing its products. The artist himself is one of nature's means, and to me Redon is one of those chosen for the continuance of its creations. His dreams become reality through the probability he gives them. All his plants, his embryonic beings, are essentially human, have lived with us. They certainly have their share of suffering. Redon speaks with his crayon. Is it matter that he is after with that inner eye? In all his work I see only the language of the heart, very human and not at all monstrous.

Redon's imagery, with its convincing unreality, its elusiveness, though stylistically related to Grandville's cartoons of half a century

111 Redon *Evocation of Roussel, c.* 1912

Redon, on the other hand, was an omnivorous reader and felt that an artist should be 'a painter in front of nature, a thinker in his studio'. Many of his themes are taken from literary sources; many writers took their themes from his works. 'What did I put in my works', he asked in *À Soi-même*, 'to suggest to young writers so many subtleties? Just a little door opening on a mystery.' His closest links were with Mallarmé, whose works he illustrated and with whom, during one period when he was living at Samois near Valvins on the outskirts of Fontainebleau, where the poet had his house, he was in almost daily contact.

Moreau, Redon, Denis and Puvis de Chavannes could rely on the mythology of Greece and Rome, as well as on the more evocative iconography of Christianity. But there were others who had to go rummaging through the detritus of ill-formulated philosophical systems and obscure religious sects to find adequately gnomic imagery to embellish their paintings and support the aesthetic apologia which underpinned them. There were certain basic notions which had a prima facie appeal. 'Evil', of various suggestive though often imprecise kinds, enjoyed a popularity which it had not known since the Middle Ages and the sinister *femmes fatales* of Félicien Rops, the ominously beguiling sphinxes of Khnopff and the menacing landscapes of Segantini suggested the revival of a form of Manicheism.

It was symptomatic of the current unpopularity of virtue that the novel which won fame for Sâr Péladan (it was the first of a series which eventually ran into forty volumes) was published in 1884 and was entitled *Le vice suprême*. We have already seen him as the originator of the Salon de la Rose + Croix, which offered exhibition space to a range of artists including Bernard, Vallotton, Filiger, Desboutin and Rouault, but this was a more unusual enterprise than might at first sight appear. Péladan had been initiated into the occult by his eldest brother Antonin in his native Lyons. When he came to Paris he became a member of the Rosicrucian sect whose obscure beliefs, which were supposed to endow them with magical powers, were based on the writings of a problematic fifteenth-century mystic, Christian Rosenkreuz. In the course of his explorations into Rosicrucian mysteries, Péladan visited the Holy Land, 'discovered' the authentic tomb of Jesus in the mosque of Omar and, with the financial backing of de la Rochefoucauld, himself a mediocre but highly allusive painter, created an order of the Rose + Croix of which the Salon was to be the show-case.

115 Rops *Pornocrates* 1896

116 Vallotton *Portrait of Thadée Natanson* 1897

117 Toulouse-Lautrec *La Revue Blanche* 1895, poster (Misia Natanson)

119 Rousseau *Eve, c.* 1905–07

The Salon refused to accept a wide variety of painting, including the patriotic, the domestic and 'all landscapes except those done in the style of Poussin', but welcomed 'even if the execution be imperfect, subjects connected with Catholic dogma, Oriental religions 'except those of the yellow races', allegories, 'sublime' nudes, murals and drawings for stained glass. On the assumption that architecture was 'killed' in 1789, it would only accept projects for fairy-tale palaces.

The Salon de la Rose + Croix represented the most outlandish aspects of the quest for the symbolic, though it might be noted that its emphasis on Poussin could well have been approved by both Cézanne and Seurat. A more significant impetus came from the world of literature in the shape of *La Revue Blanche*. Founded by the brothers Alexandre and Thadée Natanson, it was the spearhead of modernity in late nineteenth-century Paris. Tristan Bernard, Mallarmé, Valéry and de Gourmont were amongst its regular contributors and Proust had his first article published in its pages. It contained illustrations – and sometimes loose prints – by Toulouse-Lautrec, Bonnard, 105 Vuillard, Roussel, Sérusier, Denis and Vallotton. Its office in the rue 104 des Martyrs mounted exhibitions, including one by Vuillard, and was a regular meeting place for artists such as van Dongen and even Renoir. In its pages were to be found articles about the works of Cézanne, Gauguin and the Nabis and others. Some of these were from the pen of Thadée Natanson, whose house in the avenue Champs 116 Elysées, the salon of which was decorated with ten large panels by Vuillard, was a centre of Parisian life, second only to Mallarmé's flat. It was presided over by his attractive wife Misia, whom Toulouse- 117 Lautrec featured on the poster for the magazine published in 1895. Amongst those who frequented her salon were Fénéon, who became 114 the virtual editor, the young André Gide, Jarry, Léon Blum, Colette and Debussy.

The theatre played an important role in the development of the artistic as well as the literary dimensions of Post-Impressionism. A key figure in this connection was Aurélien Lugné-Poë, who had been to school with Vuillard at the Lycée Condorcet and when he was a student at the Conservatoire d'Art Dramatique shared a studio with him, Bonnard and Denis. By 1889 he had embarked on a highly successful career, first as an actor at the avant-garde Théâtre Libre and then as actor-manager of the two theatres he founded, the Théâtre d'Art and the Théâtre de l'Oeuvre. In all these capacities he publicized the work of the Nabis and others, giving them commissions for posters, programmes and stage designs. In 1895, for instance, he 120 commissioned Lautrec to provide the programme cover for a play problematically translated from the Hindustani entitled *Le Chariot de terre-cuit* and also to design sets for the fifth act, though none of them survive. Lugné-Poë was useful in other ways. In 1891 Denis wrote to him, 'I can't let this vogue for Gauguin slip by without taking advantage of it. This is the moment to introduce us to Godfroy [an influential critic] and others – call me calculating if you like – my exhibition and that of Bonnard mustn't be allowed to go unnoticed.' Lugné-Poë not only bought works by the Nabis and others but also introduced them to patrons such as the successful actor Coquelin Cadet and Jules Clarétie, the director of the Comédie Française. Moreover, the plays performed at Lugné-Poë's theatres, especially those by Maeterlinck and Ibsen, clearly influenced painters such as Vuillard to paint those circumscribed domestic interiors which parallel the settings for plays such as *The Intruder* and *The Wild Duck*.

121

A IBSEN

FV

121 Vallotton *Ibsen* 1894

120 Vuillard, programme for the Théâtre Libre, Paris, 1890

Music had a greater effect on the Post-Impressionist imagination
than it had on any earlier art form. Signac, influenced no doubt by
Whistler's use of musical terms, started to give his works opus
numbers in 1887 and, when he exhibited twelve paintings at Les XX
in 1891, provided them with musical titles – a view of ships at
Concarneau, for instance, was called *Presto (Finale)*. When he later
showed them at the Indépendants, he used more prosaic descriptive
titles. He was especially preoccupied with finding analogies between
his paintings and Wagner's harmonies. Wagner indeed was a presence
which hovered over many artists. In the 1870s, when his music first
made its impact on Paris, admiration of his works was a touchstone of
aesthetic acumen, shared by Manet, Renoir, Fantin-Latour and,
surprisingly, Cézanne, who titled a painting of a young woman
playing the piano *Overture to Tannhäuser* and seems to have been
influenced in several of his compositions, such as *Idyll* (*c.* 1870), by
Wagner's elaborate scenery for the production of the opera. The
works of Moreau, as Mario Praz has pointed out, were like the music

114

123

122 Delville *Parsifal* 1890

123 Cézanne *Overture to Tannhäuser*,
c. 1869–70

of Wagner, loaded with significant accessories in which the main theme was re-echoed until 'the subject yielded up the last drop of its symbolic sap'. A new series of Wagner productions at the Opéra in the 1880s created an even keener cult of that composer, stimulated by the publication of *La Revue Wagnérienne* – whose editor, Téodor de Wyzéva, was the lover of Jane Avril – and by enthusiastic praise from Bernard and others. In his room at Le Pouldu, Sérusier pinned up a sententious quotation from Wagner, expressing a wish that 'the faithful disciples of real art will be glorified and, surrounded by a heavenly amalgam of rays, perfumes and melodious sounds, will return to lose themselves for all eternity in the bosom of the divine source of harmony.' This was just the sort of pabulum which the Symbolist imagination craved. Wagnerian subjects became popular 122 and other themes were treated in a Wagnerian style. His music shared with the philosophy of Schopenhauer, the writings of Charles Henry and the works of an assortment of Christian and Hindu mystics the enthralled attention of every young artist in Paris.

124 Sérusier *Melancholia, c.* 1890

CHAPTER SIX

The Discredited Object

One of the central issues which vexed painters particularly in the nineteenth century had been how to define the central concern of a work of art. Was it the form or the content? Was it the purely visual effect, the resonances which certain combinations of colours, lines and composition exerted on spectators without them necessarily being able to explain or rationalize them, or was it subject matter and meaning that were paramount? It was becoming apparent that an inherent weakness in Symbolism, for instance, was that to have its total effect an image must postulate in spectators some awareness of its historical, religious, literary or even social significance. When Denis painted the Annunciation he was conscious that the majority of those who saw it would either, as French Catholics, be aware of its meaning or, as non-Catholics, know from their cultural background the 'story' behind it. Redon's *The Sleep of Caliban* would have a different effect   125 on somebody who knew the works of Shakespeare from that on somebody who didn't; when Gauguin painted a naked girl lying in a landscape with a fox nestling on her shoulder, he was giving it an additional dimension of meaning by calling it *Loss of Virginity*. One of   126 the most significant achievements of Impressionism had been to minimize, or at least appear to underplay, the necessity for such external glosses. The academic artists of the period, on the other hand, had been unable to do without them and almost invariably bolstered the effect of the conventional form of a painting with additional support, so that stories, anecdotes and the cast of history and religion were pressed into service to help establish that bond with the viewing public which they considered the central function of art. But the young men on their boating parties, the shop girls at their dances, the prostitutes at their ablutions who peopled the canvases of Renoir, Morisot and Degas were generalized figures of contemporary society, not involved in any anecdotal function – although the very choice of such subjects was not itself without meaning.

Symbolism was the most violent reaction against this 'realism' but it soon started to become apparent that it was all too likely to get

125 Redon *The Sleep of Caliban*

bogged down in iconographies so esoteric or so personal that they tended to become meaningless to the spectator. In exploring ways of establishing a psychological rapport with the spectator, some of the Post-Impressionists embarked on a journey which led, in the not too distant future, to pure abstraction and the vindication of Denis's aphorism about the nature of a painting (*see* p. 97). Colour came to play an increasingly dominant part and it was rapidly becoming 130 divorced, as Gauguin had shown in his green and yellow Christs, 74 from any descriptive function. Indeed, Cézanne had already been proving that it was taking over from line as a means of defining volume. As nobody had evolved a complete grammar of the psychological effects of colour – though Henry had made some interesting suggestions on the subject – there was no system analogous

126 Gauguin *Loss of Virginity* 1890

127 Van Gogh *Lieutenant Milliet* 1888

128 Marquet
*Sergeant of the Colonial
Army* 1907

to that which the Pointillists had evolved for its purely optical impact.
The most efficient use of colour depended on instinct in the first place
and accumulated experience in the second.

Constantly throughout his letters, van Gogh talked about colour.
In 1883 he wrote to Théo:

A painter does better to start from the colours on his palette than from the
colours in nature. I mean, when one wants to paint for instance a head, and
sharply observes the reality one has before one, then one may think: that head
is a harmony of reddish brown, violet, yellow, all of them broken – I will put
a violet, a yellow and a reddish brown on my palette, and these will break
each other.

I retain from nature a certain sequence and a certain correctness in placing
the tones. I study nature so as not to do foolish things – however I don't mind
so much whether my colour corresponds exactly, as long as it looks beautiful
on the canvas, as beautiful as it looks in nature . . . to start from one's palette,
from one's knowledge of colour harmony is quite different from following
nature obsequiously.

175

129 Laval *Self-Portrait with Landscape: à l'ami Vincent* 1888

'Looking beautiful on the canvas' had become an increasing preoccupation with younger painters and there was a growing
129 realization of van Gogh's significance. In January 1890 Aurier published a highly laudatory article about him in the *Mercure de France*, paying special attention to 'His unbelievably dazzling colour. He is, as far as I know, the only one who perceives the colouration of things with such intensity, with such a metallic gem-like quality.' In 1891 Signac organized a section devoted to his works at the Indépendants and helped Maus to organize a retrospective in Brussels at Les XX. In the following year Bernard arranged an exhibition at Le Barc de Boutteville's. One of the visitors to the latter exhibition was
128 the young Albert Marquet, whose works at this period clearly show
127 the influence of van Gogh and who was later to claim that round about this time he started painting what were to be called 'fauve' paintings. A similar impact was experienced by other young painters such as Matisse, Derain and Vlaminck.

176

130 Sérusier *The Talisman (Landscape in the Bois d'Amour)* 1888

131 Meyer de Haan *Farm at Le Pouldu* 1889

It would be naive to see van Gogh as the sole precursor of bold colour free from subordination to a descriptive or even a decorative function. Bernard himself, that constantly self-interrogative painter, had dabbled for a short time in Pointillism till he became involved in a mutually profitable relationship with Gauguin (it ended in acrimony in 1891 with both of them laying claim to having been responsible for the creation of the Pont-Aven School's approach to art). Bernard had dominated the Volpini exhibition, showing 25 works against Gauguin's 17. His *Buckwheat Harvest* – with its gradation of flame tones in the stooks, its flat area of a single red in the upper reaches of the picture, its medley of greens, bluish whites and dark shades all combined to form a series of sinuous curves which relates to those of the tree – is a remarkable example of the use of liberated colour and clearly had an effect on Gauguin's *Vision after the Sermon*. Looking back on his career, Bernard wrote in a letter to his friend Ciolkowski:

132 Filiger *Landscape at Le Pouldu* 1895

During the first period of my life I yielded to colour. I thought that brilliance was everything. At that time I was a sensuous mystic. Later I realized that the charm of colour does not lie in brilliance but in sensibility. I then reduced my palette to two colours, shading rather than colouring, and I no longer worked with complementaries but with the juxtaposition of a hot tone and a cold tone which integrates them. Finally in my third period I left as much as possible to form, and the noble, grave, austere tone has become my ideal, a kind of organ music replacing the violin of my first period.

Van Gogh saw this 'violin' phase, with its large, flat patterns of colour, as 'something deliberate, sensible, something solid and assured', and Gauguin's work, both at the time and even much later, owed a great debt to it, a debt which his more vigorous creative abilities were able to exploit more extensively. It had been he who had been responsible for promoting the notion of yet another movement, Synthetism, taken from Symbolist writings.

133 Bernard *The Buckwheat Harvest* 1888

181

Gauguin expediently used Synthetism in the publicity for the Volpini exhibition and basically it was an attempt to amalgamate emotive colour and significant form. Later this was supplanted by Pictorial Symbolism, a phrase equally designed to convey the notion of the achieved reconciliation of two potentially contradictory elements.

Sérusier had met Gauguin in the year that he himself had first exhibited at the Salon and, as a consequence of his friendship with Bernard, went to Pont-Aven where Gauguin gave him some 'lessons' in the nearby, poetically named Bois d'Amour. These resulted in painting that took the emancipation of colour much further than ever before. *The Talisman (Landscape in the Bois d'Amour)*, which precipitated the emergence of the Nabis, virtually forsook nature altogether, at least nature as the Impressionists and their immediate predecessors had known it. Great flat yellow masses of leaves, perched on light-coloured tree trunks rooted in a red bank are reflected as jagged chromatic masses in various shades of yellow, brown and very pale blue in a stream which is diversified by jagged white shapes, the whole kaleidoscope of flat colour occupying a canvas measuring only 27 by 22 centimetres. Denis, who was quick to realize the importance of the work, pointed out that 'it demonstrated that all works of art are a transposition, a caricature, the passionate equivalent of an experienced sensation.' This talk about passion and sensation was a new thing in art. By the 1890s its appeal was ubiquitous but it was not until the arrival of the Fauves in 1905 that it became sufficiently codified to be an accepted and coherent group attitude.

The subsequent career of Sérusier accented a problem which seemed always to face those who gave primacy to 'liberated colour'. Were they to try to establish as it were a colour catechism based on ideas culled from Henry or even more esoteric sources, or were they to allow themselves to be guided by more decorative considerations, which would make their work more *chic*, more palatable to the general public? Those who did a great deal of graphic work were certainly inclined to the latter. Both Bonnard and Vuillard in their works used strong, flat colours with marked elements of caricature and exaggeration but as time went by the driving force behind them became less the expression of feeling than the imposition of a pleasing pattern. Vuillard was especially conscious of the problem and suffered recurring doubts about the varying degrees of importance he should attach to line and colour, the decorative and the expressive, naturalism and stylization.

134 Carrière *Motherhood,*
c. 1890

135 Vallotton *The*
Balloon 1899

136 Matisse *Luxe, calme et volupté* 1904

It would almost seem as though the kind of decisions which artists made were, in part at least, influenced by cultural considerations. The Nabis were, almost without exception, from the upper ranks of the bourgeoisie and several of them had been to the same prestigious Parisian school, the Lycée Condorcet. As such they belonged to a very specific stratum of French culture, rooted in the classical tradition, moulded by Descartes and Voltaire (the Marquis de Condorcet, after whom the school was named, had been a philosopher and the author of *L'Esquisse d'un tableau historique du progrès de l'ésprit humain*) and dedicated to imposing rational control over the more wayward manifestations of creativity. The more uninhibited exponents of the free use of colour and the primacy of feeling tended to come from different cultures or different social backgrounds: van Gogh and van Dongen were Dutch, Gauguin of mixed Spanish, Peruvian and French blood; Vlaminck of Flemish descent was a racing cyclist before he took to painting; Matisse, Valtat, Dufy, Freisz were all from the extreme north of France. The most enthusiastic welcome to the work of the colourist element in Post-Impressionism came from Belgium and its most dedicated disciples, who were to extend its principles into Expressionism, came from Germany and the northern countries.

136

137 Van de Velde
Woman at a Window 1890

Typical of the kind of influence which Post-Impressionism exerted by the revolution in the meaning and use of colour is the career of the Norwegian Edvard Munch, who spent lengthy periods in Paris between 1888 and 1896. His earlier fixation on Impressionism was supplanted by the influence on his work of Gauguin, Bernard, van Gogh and the Nabis, thus enabling him to develop an art dominated by the use of emotive colour and the bounding, expressive lines which characterized the work of the more experimental elements in French painting at the time. Equally significant was the Belgian Henry van de Velde, musician, architect, painter and designer, who was a regular exhibitor at the Indépendants, a friend and occasionally an imitator of the Pointillists. He decorated the offices of *La Revue Blanche* and was a significant intermediary between French and German painting and the decorative arts of the period.

The implicit schism between those who were concerned with the primacy of pure colours and those who were more concerned with

subject matter, with symbolic associations, with decorative patterns or with the structured realization of formal values was bound sooner or later to become codified by the creation of one of those movements or groups which had become so essential to art life of the time. This happened at the Salon d'Automne of 1905 when the word 'fauve' was coined by an imaginative critic – Vauxcelles – just as the word 'Impressionist' had been. All those who were to be so called had developed methods of painting and approaches to the use of colour which had been practised not only by van Gogh, Sérusier, Bernard and even by Redon (in works such as *Portrait of Gauguin*) but had also been theorized about by Signac, whose meeting with Matisse and Cross in the summer of 1904 was to have a definitive effect on his attitudes. Matisse and Marquet had worked together as students, first at the École des Arts Décoratifs, then at the École des Beaux-Arts, where they studied under Moreau, whose teaching, according to Matisse, they found deeply disturbing.

139

138 Munch *The Dance of Life* 1899

139 Redon *Portrait of Gauguin* 1904

140 Derain *Effects of Sun on Water* 1905

140   After leaving the École, Matisse met André Derain, who at this
time was living at Chatou, that shrine of Impressionism, near
141   Vlaminck, and the two shared a studio. Their coherence as a group
was cemented by the impact of the van Gogh exhibition of 1891. At
142   the same time, three young artists from Le Havre, Raoul Dufy,
143, 144   Othon Friesz and Georges Braque, who had all attended evening
classes at the École Municipale des Beaux-Arts, formed what they
called, rather optimistically, the Le Havre group.

Dominated by Matisse, the members of the whole group were fired
with the enthusiasm which they expressed in their painting. As Derain
was later to recall:

It was the age of photography, and that may have influenced us, and
contributed to anything which remotely resembled a photograph taken

188

141 Vlaminck *La Seine à Chatou* 1905

from life. We treated colour like sticks of dynamite, exploding them to produce light. The idea that everything could be elevated above reality was marvellous in its pristine freshness. The great thing about our experiment was that it freed painting from all imitative or conventional contexts. We attacked colour directly.

They were full of initiative. Matisse and Marquet exhibited regularly at the Indépendants from 1901 onwards and they had made their appearance at the Salon d'Automne two years before they had acquired their name as a group. Moreover, they had found dealers who were interested in their work. Chief amongst them was the enterprising Berthe Weill, who had a tiny gallery in the rue Victor-Massé. She had started exhibiting Matisse and Marquet in 1902 and the others in the following years, introducing them to van Dongen.

189

Then there was the Druet Gallery, which had opened in the rue du Faubourg-St-Honoré in 1903; it mounted exhibitions of Signac and Cross and showed the work of Matisse and Derain. Another outlet was provided by Pierre Soulier, a junk dealer and mattress carder in the rue des Martyrs, who had an eye for art as sharp as Père Tanguy's; he had been one of the first to sell works by the Douanier Rousseau and was quick to adopt these new painters.

Although much of the publicity which the group received at the Salon d'Automne in 1905 was hostile, an appreciable amount was friendly. A special feature in *L'Illustration*, illustrating works by Matisse, Derain, Valtat and others, though it may have been intended to ridicule both critics and artists, probably had the opposite effect.

There were two particularly astute comments on the work of the Fauves. One from Thiébault-Sisson in *Le Temps* for 17 October 1905 stressed a new influence:

The ideal to which a section in the battalion of young artists recently aspires involved recapturing the soul of a young child – that of a small child who has never seen any images – to look at nature and life with sincerity and to interpret both with greater naïveté. But unless one is a primitive or disturbed, it is difficult to keep the soul of a small child when one reaches maturity; it is even more difficult to recapture it once one has lost it.

The art of children did indeed have a significance for the Fauves. The primitive art forms which had appealed to so many of the earlier Post-Impressionists were equally potent influences on the younger generation. In 1904 Vlaminck bought two negro sculptures and his example was followed by Derain and Matisse. At the same time artists became aware of the artistic sensibilities of children, especially in that stage of their creative growth when they represent things not according to sight but by reason, with visual incongruities, the use of conventional instead of imitative elements, bright, vivid non–realistic colouring and two dimensions instead of three. 'A thing which bothers me', said Derain once, 'is drawing. I would like to study children's drawings. That's where the truth lies, without a doubt.' When in 1905 he painted a portrait of Vlaminck, the picture possessed a child-like quality in the simplified outline of the face and hat, the prominence given to the eyes and the truncated moustache.

The other most significant comment, which perhaps went some way to explaining why the Fauves as a group did not survive much beyond 1908, came from Denis, who wrote in *L'Ermitage* of December 1906 about the works of Matisse:

145 Derain *Portrait of Vlaminck* 1905

Of course, as in the most extravagant flights of van Gogh, something still remains of the original feeling for nature. But here one finds, above all in the work of Matisse, the sense of the artificial; not the literary artificial, like the search for idealistic expression; nor that of decorative artificiality such as one sees in Turkish and Persian carpet weavers; no, it is something even more abstract; it is painting above every contingency, painting in itself, the pure act of painting. All the qualities of the picture, other than the contrasts of light and colour, everything which the rational mind of the painter has not controlled, everything which comes from instinct and from nature, finally all the factors of representation and of feeling, are excluded from the work of art. Yet, strange contradiction, this absolute is limited by the one thing in the world that is most relative: individual emotion.

146 Matisse *Les Toits de Collioure* 1906

Art had been a good deal easier for the Impressionists. They had simply been concerned with expressing, admittedly in a novel way, their comprehension and reactions to what they saw, mostly in nature. They were untroubled by questions of inner meaning; decorative conceptions troubled them not at all. Nature was a treasure trove to be rifled to reflect a kind of optimistic materialism which demanded little else from the spectator but contemplation. Now things were very different. The picture had become an autonomous object, an arrangement of coloured forms which transformed the world as it appeared into a reality in the mind of the spectator. 'Art', as Cézanne said, 'is a harmony parallel to nature.' Painting had become a dialogue among the artist, the spectator and the thing painted. Colour began to lose all descriptive function. When Matisse was working at

Collioure in the company of Signac and Cross he painted out-of-doors views such as that of the town roofs but the grass, the hills and the outlines of the harbour were all red and scattered over the whole work are patches of green and turquoise, their shapes largely determined by the accent of the brush-stroke on the canvas. At the same time Matisse was deeply conscious – as were Cézanne and the Pointillists – of the necessity of finding a form of expression, as in his masterpiece of this period, *Luxe, calme et volupté*, in which objects, forms and abstraction are united to convey a state of mind. It seemed almost at times as though the object as it had been known in European painting was either going to disappear or be so transformed as to strip it of all the associations which it possessed. As he put it himself in 'Notes d'un peintre' in 1908:

The painter's idea cannot be conceived apart from the means he uses, for it is meaningful only so far as it is embodied in those means, and the deeper his idea, the more complete they must be. I an unable to distinguish between my feelings for life and my way of transposing it. A painting must carry all its meanings within itself, and impose it on the viewer before he identifies the subject matter.

There were already echoes of this sentiment in the works of that most Impressionist of Impressionists, Monet, in whose 'series' paintings hayricks and cathedrals were starting to merge into a background of broken colours, vigorous brushwork and thickly textured paint so as to become almost invisible. It was one of Monet's hayricks which, when he saw it at a Moscow exhibition in 1895, provided the 29-year-old Wassily Kandinsky with the revelation that was to make him one of the pioneers of an objectless art:

Suddenly, for the first time, I saw a 'picture'. The catalogue told me that it was a hayrick but I could not recognize it. This lack of recognition was distressing. I also felt that the artist had no right to paint so indistinctly. I had a muffled sense that the object was lacking in this picture and was overcome with astonishment and perplexity that it not only seized but engraved itself indelibly on the memory and quite unexpectedly, again and again hovered before the eyes down to the smallest detail . . . What was absolutely clear to me was the unsuspected power, previously hidden from me, of the palette, which surpassed all my dreams. Painting took on a fabulous strength and splendour. And at the same time the object was discredited as an indispensable element of the picture.

There could hardly be a better way of summing up the nature of Post-Impressionism. It emphasizes in the first place, as Kandinsky's revelation came through Monet's painting, that, though its exponents

146

136

147
148

147 Monet *Haystacks* 1890–91

saw themselves as revolting against their predecessors, many of them, ranging from Seurat to Matisse, were exploiting elements implicit in Impressionism. The first steps to the liberation of colour were in fact present in the very painting by Monet which had given the earlier movement its name. Many of them, though in a more overtly political form, continued the preoccupation with the realities of contemporary life which had led critics such as Zola to prefer the word 'Realists' to that of 'Impressionists' and it was a preoccupation which would continue in various styles of painting for another century. The 'discrediting of the object', as Kandinsky called it, was one of the main contributions of Post-Impressionism to the art of the future, leading to Expressionism, abstraction and the combination of

148 Kandinsky *Blue Mountain* 1908

the two in America in the middle of the twentieth century. On the other hand, the object was also canonized in the monumentality of Cézanne and the Pointillists, just as it was to be in the art of Cubism and the various forms of 'magic realism' such as the Neue Sachlichkeit ('New Objectivity'). The Symbolist elements, naive as they sometimes seemed, were to be intellectualized and vigorized by Freudian dialectics to power Surrealism and its derivatives. In opening up the future of painting in this way, the generation which, to use an oversimplified metaphor, 'took over' from Impressionism had underlined the emergence of the work of art as an independent object. As Denis pointed out in his *Journal*, 'Some pushed it all the way to abstraction; others all the way back to the museum.'

Biographies

Allais, Alphonse (1855–1905) Journalist and writer of Norman origin, who at the exhibition of the Incohérents in 1882 showed a sheet of white board entitled *The First Communion of Anaemic Young Girls in the Snow*. Now in the Musée des Arts Décoratifs in Paris, it could be regarded as the first example of Dada art.

Aman-Jean, Edmond (1860–1936) A fellow student of Seurat at Jehmann's studio, he also worked under Puvis de Chavannes, whom he assisted in the painting of *The Sacred Grove* (1884). Seurat's portrait drawing of him was shown at the Salon of 1883. Apart from exhibiting at the various Salons, he also showed works at the Salon de la Rose + Croix in 1892 and 1893. His later work was deeply influenced by Bonnard.

Angrand, Charles (1854–1926) Educated in Rouen and starting his artistic career under the influence of Bastien-Lepage, he soon became an Impressionist and then, under the influence of Seurat and Signac, a Pointillist. In close contact with van Gogh, he exhibited at the Salon des Indépendants and with the Artistes Incohérents. In 1896 he returned to Normandy and virtually gave up painting.

Anquetin, Louis (1861–1932) Like Toulouse-Lautrec, he studied first under Bonnat and then under Cormon, in whose studio, which he came to dominate, he met Bernard and van Gogh. A forceful and intellectually vital person, he commenced as an Impressionist under the influence of Monet but then, in collaboration with Bernard, evolved a style which the critic Dujardin dubbed Cloisonnism – marked by emphatic black lines, flat colour areas and a strong undercurrent of Symbolism. He was influenced at various times by Degas, Toulouse-Lautrec, Japanese prints and stained-glass windows. By the end of the 80s, however, he abandoned these more innovative experiments for a kind of monumental style based predominantly on Rubens.

Aurier, Georges Albert (1871–1932) Painter and critic, he met Bernard at Saint-Briac in Brittany in 1888 and was introduced by him to his painter friends. He became especially appreciative of van Gogh, about whom he wrote a laudatory article in the *Mercure de France* in January 1890 and another on Gauguin a year later in the same journal, in which he defined Symbolism. His complete criticism was published posthumously in 1893.

Bernard, Émile (1868–1941) A pupil at Cormon's studio, like Anquetin and Toulouse-Lautrec, but was expelled for 'unruly behaviour' and went to paint in Normandy. There he met Gauguin at Pont-Aven and became very close to him in the period between 1888 and 1892, when he evolved a doctrine of Pictorial Symbolism, which led the older artist to paint his *Vision after the Sermon*. He had previously passed through Impressionist, Pointillist and Cloisonnist phases. When Gauguin went to Tahiti Bernard fell under the influence of the Nabis and exhibited at the first Salon de la Rose + Croix exhibition in 1892 and at Le Barc de Boutteville's in the same year and the one following. At the end of 1883 he went to Egypt where he stayed until 1904, returning to develop an academic style. On his return he went to visit Cézanne and wrote a number of illuminating, if not always textually accurate, accounts of the experience, later collected into book form. He was a prolific writer about the artists of his generation. He became obsessed in his latter years with disclaiming the influence of Gauguin.

Bevan, Robert (1865–1925) The son of a Brighton banker, he studied at the Westminster School of Art for two years and then enrolled at the Académie Julian, where he met Bonnard, Vuillard, Denis and Sérusier. He made several visits to Brittany and in 1893 stayed at the Villa Julia in Pont-Aven and became friendly with Gauguin, who dedicated a monotype, *Two Standing Tahitian Women*, to him. Bevan's prints during this period were very deeply influenced by Gauguin's Synthetism. He developed a personal style marked by long, flowing lines and surface patternings reminiscent of the work of van Gogh. He settled in London in 1900 and later became involved in the Camden Town Group and the London Group, both hotbeds of Post-Impressionist tendencies in British art.

Bing, Samuel (1853–1905) An art dealer who in 1895 opened a gallery in Paris which specialized in Japanese works. In 1902 he turned to contemporary art and design at a new gallery in the rue de Provence, which showed works by Rodin, Denis, Bonnard, Vuillard, Sérusier, Ranson and Toulouse-Lautrec, as well as glasswork by Tiffany and furniture by Van de Velde.

Bonnard, Pierre (1867–1947) Son of a senior civil servant, after passing his law degrees he became a student at the École des Beaux-Arts and the Académie Julian, where he met Denis and Sérusier, whose work had a powerful influence on him, as did Japanese art and Gauguin. He shared a studio with Vuillard. In the 1890s he exhibited at the Salon des Indépendants and Le Barc de Boutteville's. Like all the Nabis he was involved in the applied arts, designing panels, screens, stained glass and furniture. He was also very much a graphic artist, closely connected with the avant-garde magazine *La Revue Blanche*, and created stage designs, notably for the first production of *Ubu Roi* in 1896. His very personal style contained elements derived from a number of sources but *c.* 1915 he revised it in the direction of a modified Impressionism. It was on work of this kind that his later reputation as a 'pure painter' depended.

Bouguereau, Adolphe (1825–1905) A pillar of the French art establishment and a firm opponent of all innovation, he achieved enormous popularity mainly through engravings of his works, which were usually on religious, mythological and historic themes.

Boussod & Valadon In 1875 the firm of Goupil was taken over by Etienne Boussod, who was married to Goupil's grand-daughter,

and a man named Valadon, who sacked Vincent van Gogh from his job in the London branch but continued to employ Théo van Gogh at their gallery in Montmartre. There Théo supported as best he could the Impressionists and younger painters such as Gauguin.

Camoin, Charles (1879–1965) Born in Marseilles, he came to the École des Beaux-Arts where he worked under Moreau and met Marquet and Matisse. In 1901 he met Cézanne and remained in close contact with him, later publishing a series of the master's statements about art. Although a Fauve, painting mainly landscapes and figures, predominantly in the Mediterranean area, his ingeniously composed work lacks the spontaneous vibrancy of the painters he most admired, such as Derain and Matisse.

Carrière, Eugène (1849–1906) Born in Strasbourg and trained in lithography, the textures and tonal qualities of that medium always affected his work. Coming to Paris he studied at the École des Beaux-Arts under Cabanel but kept himself by working in the studios of the poster artist Jules Chéret. Until the end of the 1880s he practised a predominantly naturalistic style centred on scenes of family life. Then his work assumed a strangely mysterious quality, with strong symbolic undercurrents, and he was taken up by authors such as Mallarmé and Verlaine. He exchanged works with Gauguin and became a cult figure to a whole generation of artists.

Cézanne, Paul (1839–1906) Although, almost by accident, one of the founding fathers of Impressionism, Cézanne was never really a convinced or convincing exponent of its ideals and techniques and, especially after his withdrawal to Aix-en-Provence in the late 1870s, was far more concerned with form and structure, using colour as a means of reinforcing them rather than as a description of light and atmosphere. His work was largely disregarded until an exhibition at Vollard's in 1895 revealed to a younger generation how much they owed him, an idea vigorously promoted by Bernard and Denis. Gauguin was greatly influenced by him.

Chéret, Jules (1836–1933) Beginning his career as a commercial artist in Paris, he moved to London for eight years, where he acquired a knowledge of the latest developments in lithographic printing. When he returned to Paris in 1866 he transformed poster art, introducing brilliant colour schemes and flowing rococo lines which attracted the attention and won the approval of nearly all artistic schools of thought. He employed the visual language of popular folk art to produce imagery that accustomed people to artistic innovations which they would have rejected in a more formal context. Lautrec owed a great deal to him and he was admired by most avant-garde artists.

Cross, Henri-Edmond (1856–1910) When he arrived in Paris from Douai in 1881 Cross was painting in an Impressionist style but ten years later he was converted to Pointillism, which he used with decorative freedom. He spent most of the rest of his painting career in the south. A committed Socialist with anarchist leanings, his paintings had a certain Utopian quality about them.

Dagnan-Bouveret, Pascal (1852–1929) He started exhibiting at the Salon in 1875 and was applauded for the minute realism of his paintings, often on domestic themes, some with a Breton background. He had strong inclinations to Symbolism, especially in his mural paintings.

Delvallée, Henri (1862–1943) Painter and print-maker, he lived and worked in Pont-Aven for several years, where he taught Armand Seguin the art of etching. He practised both Pointillist and Divisionist styles, and many of his works were on Breton themes.

Denis, Maurice (1870–1943) Having studied at the École des Beaux-Arts, he was a founder member of the Nabis. In the 1890s he exhibited at the Salon des Indépendants and Le Barc de Boutteville's and worked in a wide range of media: book illustration, prints, decorative art, theatre design, stained glass and costume designs. An inveterate theoretician, he wrote about art extensively and set about reviving Christian art mainly through the Ateliers d'Art Sacré. His two most important books are *Théories* (1912) and *Nouvelles Théories* (1922).

Durand-Ruel, Paul (1831–1922) The son of a picture dealer, he inherited the business in 1865. Five years later, having moved to London to escape the Franco-Prussian war and its aftermath, he met there Pissarro and Monet and started a life-long connection with the Impressionists which worked to the advantage of both. He was especially successful in opening up to them the American market. He also sold and promoted works by van Gogh, Gauguin and the Nabis.

Ensor, James (1860–1949) A Belgian painter of partly English descent who lived most of his life in Ostend. After studying at the Académie Royale des Beaux-Arts in Brussels, he came into contact with avant-garde and radical movements. He was a founder member of Les XX and later of La Libre Esthétique. Commencing within the framework of traditional Impressionism, he developed a highly personal style with recurrent themes of masks, fish and skeletons, which looked back to Bosch and Bruegel and forwards to Surrealism.

Fénéon, Félix (1861–1944) The most influential and sagacious critic of the whole period of Post-Impressionism, Fénéon was actively involved with the Neo-Impressionists, the Symbolists and figures such as Gauguin and Lautrec. As an editor he published writers such as Mallarmé and Rimbaud. He was a passionate believer in anarchism and is reputed, with some justification, to have been involved in bomb incidents.

Filiger, Charles (1863–1928) After studying art at Colarossi's in Paris, Filiger, who had been born in Alsace of Swiss parentage, went to Le Pouldu in Brittany where he met Gauguin,

Laval, Sérusier and others, by whom he was deeply influenced. Spending the rest of his life in Brittany, he became profoundly religious and his art imbued medieval and Byzantine motifs and styles. He committed suicide at the age of 65.

Forain, Jean (1852–1931) A political and social cartoonist in the tradition of Daumier, he exhibited at four of the Impressionist exhibitions, though his palette was too subdued to rank him as one of the group. His work influenced Toulouse-Lautrec, with whom he was friendly, and he himself was a great admirer of Degas.

Fry, Roger (1866–1934) English art critic and painter, closely associated with the Bloomsbury Group. He was an ardent Francophile and exerted through his writings an influence on English taste second only to that of Ruskin. His most important works were *Vision and Design* (1920) and *Transformations* (1926).

Gauguin, Paul (1848–1903) In some ways the archetypal Post-Impressionist since, even more so than Seurat's, his early career had been embedded in Impressionism and yet his evolution from it was spectacular and far-reaching. With a charismatic and domineering personality, his influence was more pervasive than specific. To the forefront in liberating colour from any representational function, he had a yearning, typical of his time, for the simple, 'natural' life which he thought he had found first in Brittany, then in Tahiti. 'Here', he said, 'I have escaped everything that is artificial and conventional. Here I enter into Truth and become one with Nature.' Despite the trivialization of his life by Somerset Maugham and lesser writers, he is in many ways a dominant figure in the evolution of twentieth-century painting.

Geffroy, Gustave (1855–1926) Novelist, journalist of radical tendencies and art critic, he was an early and perceptive supporter of Impressionism. His articles about the fine arts were published in the eight volumes of *La Vie artistique* between 1892 and 1903, the third being devoted to the history of Impressionism.

Gervex, Henri (1852–1929) An academic artist who was a friend of Monet and Renoir. He painted realistic pictures of contemporary life, including a painting of a famous surgeon performing an operation, which prompted Toulouse-Lautrec to do two paintings on the same theme in 1891.

Gogh, Vincent van (1853–90) Deciding to become a painter at the age of 22, he applied himself to the task with extraordinary involvement and incessant work. The increasing tensions in his much publicized life have tended to dilute his real achievements as an artist. Having experimented with Impressionism and Pointillism, he evolved a very personal style with crisply accented colour, strongly rhythmic forms and usually a heavy impasto. Later Expressionists owed a great deal to his innovations.

Goupil, Adolphe (1806–93) In 1827 he opened a gallery in Montmartre specializing in the sale of prints and started buying and selling works by contemporary artists. In the 1860s he was joined by Vincent van Gogh – the uncle of the painter – who had a gallery in The Hague. By the end of the decade the firm had branches in Paris, London, Brussels, Berlin and New York, the latter eventually taken over by its manager Michael Knoedler.

Guillaumin, Armand (1841–1927) A civil servant who painted when he could, he was a dedicated Impressionist who exhibited at most of the joint exhibitions and at the Salon d'Automne. Close to Cézanne and Pissarro, he also worked with Signac and was a great help to the younger generation of the 1880s, especially Seurat, Gauguin and van Gogh.

Hayet, Louis (1864–1940) A self-taught artist who had been a house-painter, he studied colour theories and became a confirmed Pointillist in the 1880s. Although he exhibited at Le Barc de Boutteville's in the later 1890s, he abandoned innovative painting at the turn of the century.

Henry, Charles (c. 1860–c. 1920) A scientist and philosopher who evolved theories about the inter-relationship of the arts and the connection between aesthetic and physiological problems. These were expounded in his *Cercle chromatique* (1888), *Rapporteur esthétique* of the same year and *Éducation des senses des formes* (1890). He had a great influence on Signac, Gauguin and the Symbolists.

Hodler, Ferdinand (1853–1918) Beginning as a painter of tourist pictures, by the 1880s he had become a fully committed Symbolist, very much under the influence of Puvis de Chavannes. He elaborated a theory of what he called 'Eurhrythmy', which involved carefully composed and orchestrated gestures of a symbolic kind made by figures in frieze-like rows, and was clearly influenced by contemporary dance movements. He was a regular exhibitor at the Salons de la Rose + Croix.

Huysmans, Joris-Karl (1848–1907) Novelist and art critic whose approach to painting was literary rather than visual. Commencing as a Realist, he is famous largely for two works published in the 1890s, *À Rebours* and *Là-bas*, which became the bibles of the younger generation of writers and painters, especially the Symbolists. He was appreciative of the works of Cézanne, Moreau and Redon, about all of whom he wrote eloquently. In his later years he had a religious conversion.

Khnopff, Fernand (1858–1921) Born in Brussels, he studied in Paris with Moreau and in 1883 was one of the group Les Vingt. A follower of Sâr Péladan, he became a leader of the Belgian Symbolist movement. After about 1890, however, he lived an isolated life in Bruges.

Laval, Charles (1862–94) An ardent disciple of Gauguin, with whose paintings his own are often confused, he worked in Pont-Aven and travelled with him to Martinique. He showed at the Café Volpini exhibition in 1889 but his

tuberculosis forced him to go to Egypt, where he died.

Luce, Maximilien (1858–1941) Starting as an engraver, he moved to painting in his mid-twenties and came under the influence of the Pointillists, whose style, sometimes in a modified form, he used for the rest of his career. A convinced and a convicted anarchist, his choice of subject matter was largely dictated by his political sympathies. Through his friendship with the Belgian poet Verhaeren, he became very interested in the industrial area around Charleroi and produced a series of paintings emphasizing the devastation of rural life by industrial development.

Maillol, Aristide (1861–1944) Although known primarily as a sculptor, a medium to which he turned in the 1890s as a result of failing eyesight, Maillol started as a painter. Originally under the influence of Puvis de Chavannes and then of Gauguin, he joined the Nabis. He had a one-man exhibition of paintings at Vollard's in 1902.

Martin, Henri (1860–1943) After studying at the École des Beaux-Arts, he took to Neo-Impressionism in 1889, combining its technique with a penchant for idealistic themes of the kind favoured by Puvis de Chavannes. He was especially interested in monumental and decorative painting.

Matisse, Henri (1869–1954) Trained as a lawyer, he took up painting in 1895, studying at the École des Beaux-Arts under Moreau. He then worked under Carrière, in whose studio he met Derain. His early works, some painted in Brittany, were Impressionistic but c. 1898, when working in Corsica, and partly as a result of reading Signac's *D'Eugène Delacroix au néo-impressionnisme*, he became more interested in the use of colour, which he applied in a loosely Neo-Impressionist way. By 1905, however, in collaboration with Derain, he abandoned this technique and started to give his colours a greater luminosity which created the effect of light without imitating it. To this he added a concern with structure derived from Cézanne. His works exhibited in the Salon d'Automne of 1905, along with those of Derain, Braque, Dufy and others, helped to create Fauvism.

Maufra, Maxime (1861–1918) A Breton by birth, he began work as a businessman but, meeting Gauguin at Pont-Aven in 1890, moved to Paris to become a painter. His style was closely influenced by that of Gauguin, with whom he was in frequent contact during the 1890s. He had a penchant for what he described as 'Symbolist landscapes', which involved a synthesis of feeling rather than of form. He was taken up by Durand-Ruel and was a very active print-maker.

Maus, Octave (1860–1913?) Lawyer, musician, journalist, art critic and man of means, Maus dominated the art world of Belgium for some twenty years. In 1881 with Edmond Picard he founded the magazine *La Vie Moderne*, which was to advocate all that was most advanced in art, music and literature. On its creation in 1884 he became the secretary and virtual director of the group known as Les Vingt whose exhibitions were representative of all that was of interest in contemporary European art.

Meyer de Haan, Jacob (1852–95) A dedicated disciple of Gauguin who praised his work in a letter to van Gogh, he lived with him for two years at Le Pouldu in Brittany from 1889 and gave him considerable financial support. The son of a rich Amsterdam merchant, he had met Gauguin and van Gogh when, shortly after his arrival in Paris, he had stayed with Théo van Gogh. He intended accompanying Gauguin to Tahiti but was unable to do so as his family cut off his allowance.

Monfreid, Georges Daniel de (1856–1929) An affluent, yacht-owning painter, who had left his wife to take up art and was a close friend and supporter of Gauguin, who pushed his work, inviting him, for instance, to exhibit at the Café Volpini. He was also a close friend of Maillol. His correspondence with Gauguin in Tahiti is important for the information it gives about Gauguin and the Parisian art world of the time.

Moreau, Gustave (1826–98) The teacher of most of the Fauves, Moreau, though belonging to a generation which had doted on Delacroix and Chassériau, had a considerable influence on many different aspects of Post-Impressionism. An intelligent and sympathetic teacher, his own work was literary in inspiration and appealed greatly to writers such as Huysmans, Mallarmé and Oscar Wilde. His style was richly ornate and exotic.

Moret, Henry (1856–1913) After commencing as an Impressionist, he joined Gauguin at Pont-Aven in 1888 and in the following year worked with the group at Le Pouldu. Besotted with the magic of the Breton landscape, he initially adopted a Gauguinesque style of painting but later reverted to Impressionism.

Munch, Edvard (1863–1944) Norwegian painter who after early studies in Oslo travelled extensively, especially in Germany and France. He first arrived in Paris in 1885 and was influenced by Impressionism and then by the Post-Impressionists, particularly van Gogh, Gauguin and Toulouse-Lautrec. In 1908 he had a mental breakdown and spent the rest of his life in Norway. He was an essential link between Post-Impressionism and outright Expressionism.

Natanson, Alexandre (1867–1936) and **Thadée** (1868–1951) Rich brothers, who founded *La Revue Blanche*, the leading journal of the Symbolist movement in art, literature and music. They were enthusiastic and generous patrons, who gave support and encouragement to a wide range of painters.

Pissarro, Camille (1830–1903) One of the founding members of the Impressionist movement and always very active in their affairs. Constantly pragmatic about his own work, he adopted a Pointillist style for a short period in 1885.

Pissarro, Lucien (1863–1944) The eldest son of Camille, he took to Neo-Impressionism at about the same time as his father and exhibited at the Indépendants and Les XX. In 1890 he moved to London and founded the Eragny Press four years later. He was responsible for spreading many of the practices of Post-Impressionism in England as a member of the Fitzroy Street Group, the Camden Town Group and the London Group.

Puvis de Chavannes, Pierre (1824–98) Studying under Delacroix and Couture, he was influenced by Chassériau's decorations for the Cours de Comptes in Paris into dedicating himself very largely to mural and decorative painting. Entirely uninfluenced by Impressionism, he was tolerant and catholic in his tastes. He favoured placid mythological and symbolic subjects and was greatly admired, though seldom imitated, by the younger artists of the last quarter of the century.

Raffaëlli, Jean-François (1850–1924) A close friend of Degas, who introduced him to the Impressionists, in whose exhibitions he participated. He specialized in paintings of the impoverished suburbs of Paris. He exhibited in Brussels with Les Vingt and eventually had considerable popular success. He made some important innovations in the art of colour printing.

Ranson, Paul (1862–1909) Painter, decorator, graphic artist and ceramicist, he studied at the École des Arts Décoratifs and the Académie Julian, where he met Sérusier, Roussel, Bonnard and Vuillard. They used to meet together at his studio to discuss aesthetics and philosophy; from these meetings emerged the Nabis. Interested in the union of the fine and decorative arts, he founded in 1908 the Académie Ranson at which Sérusier, Vallotton and Van Rysselberghe taught.

Redon, Odilon (1840–1916) Another important figure untouched by Impressionism, he devoted himself for a period of some twenty years to charcoal drawings and lithographs which had a mysterious and almost hypnotic quality. In about 1895, however, he reverted to colour used in an explosive and uninhibited way, which increased the already considerable following he had amongst the younger generation. 'The only aim of my art', he once wrote, 'is to produce within the spectator a sort of diffuse but powerful affinity with the world of the indeterminate.'

Rodin, August (1840–1917) The most successful experimental sculptor of his time, he was basically Romantic in style but was very interested in literary and symbolic associations and in the dance. A prolific watercolourist, he was friendly with several of the Post-Impressionists.

Rops, Félicien (1830–98) Born in Belgium but spent most of his working life in France. His often erotic and always fantastic illustrations were very popular. Closely linked with the Symbolists, he illustrated the works of Péladan.

Rousseau, Henri, 'Le Douanier' (1844–1910) Starting as a saxophonist in a military band and seeing service in Mexico, he became a minor official in the Parisian customs service. He took up painting in 1885, largely as a means of supplementing his meagre pension, and in the following year was introduced by Signac to the Société des Artistes Indépendants, at whose exhibitions he regularly showed his works and where he came into contact with Gauguin, Pissarro and Seurat. Amongst his admirers were Renoir, Redon, Toulouse-Lautrec and Picasso.

Roussel, Ker-Xavier (1867–1944) A fellow student of Vuillard, Roussel was one of the first members of the Nabis but he was not very much involved in group activities, though his style was very close to that of Vuillard, whose sister he married. He became interested in painting large-scale decorative panels and sensuous semi-mythological scenes.

Rysselberghe, Théo van (1862–1926) A Belgian artist who was a founder member of Les XX and La Libre Esthétique, he early adopted

204

Neo-Impressionism and became a link between its French practitioners and others in Europe through Les XX. He also designed furniture and other forms of decorative art, working in collaboration with Van de Velde.

Schuffenecker, Émile (1851–1934) A stock-broker, he worked in the same firm as Gauguin and became his devoted and supportive disciple. He spent a good deal of time at Pont-Aven and, because of the financial help he gave Gauguin, who often treated him as a door-mat, he was well represented at the Café Volpini exhibition in 1889. He was responsible for introducing Bernard to Gauguin, at a time when he himself was painting Neo-Impressionist paintings, and played a significant role in the evolution of Symbolism.

Séguin, Armand (1869?–1903) A Breton by birth, he was converted to Gauguin's style as a result of his visit to the Café Volpini exhibition in 1889. Two years later he held his own first one-man show at Le Barc de Boutteville. Supported by Sérusier, he died of tuberculosis.

Sérusier, Paul (1864–1927) Commencing briefly as an academic painter, he had the inevitable encounter with Gauguin at Pont-Aven and received lessons from him. The result of these was a painting of 1888 known as *The Talisman*, which became the pictorial manifesto of the Nabis and the centre of heated discussions about the nature of art and Symbolism, themes which were to exercise Sérusier for most of his life. He later became involved in the 'sacred' art of the Benedictine monks of Beuron in Germany. His was a powerful, intelligent mind and he influenced a number of artists and critics.

Seurat, Georges (1859–91) Born of a well-to-do family, after studying at the École des Beaux-Arts, he devoted his early efforts to precise tonal drawings influenced by Ingres and Puvis de Chavannes. At the same time, too, he was increasingly preoccupied with colour theories and the desire to reduce to a system the discoveries made instinctively by Corot, the Impressionists and others. This resulted in Pointillism or Divisionism. He then turned his attention to evolving a method for systematizing the expression of emotion through pictorial means, but died at the age of 32.

Signac, Paul (1863–1935) First an Impressionist, he was converted to Pointillism when he met Seurat in 1884 and helped found the Salon des Indépendants. On the death of Seurat he became the leader of the group and published what was virtually its text-book, *D'Eugène Delacroix au néo-impressionnisme*. There were many inconsistencies in his attempts to rationalize the use of colour and his own creative gifts were too turbulent easily to be confined within a formula. He was a convinced anarchist.

Steinlen, Théophile-Alexandre (1859–1923) Born in Lausanne, he settled in Paris and became one of the most significant graphic artists of his period, intimate with the cabaret life of Montmartre and the publications connected with it. He also produced some striking posters. He was a dedicated anarchist concerned in much of his work with social injustices.

Tanguy, Julien, 'Père' (1825–94) Fifth child of a plasterer, he first worked on the railways and then got a job with a firm of artists' colourmen, Chez Edouard. Involved in the Commune of 1871, he was imprisoned at Brest and released through the good offices of the industrialist and patron of the Impressionists Edouard Rouart. In 1873 he opened his own shop in the rue Clauzel. He rapidly attracted the custom of Cézanne, Pissarro, Guillaumin, Gauguin and van Gogh, whose pictures he sold, exhibited and promoted without any concern for making a profit.

Toulouse-Lautrec, Henri de (1864–1901) Born of an aristocratic family, virtually a dwarf as the result of a hereditary disease, an alcoholic and probably syphilitic, Toulouse-Lautrec produced a very large number of finely executed paintings, prints, posters and drawings in the course of his short life. More than anyone else he accustomed the general public to the non-veristic aspects of contemporary art through his graphic work and was a potent force in liberating colour from its descriptive functions.

Vallotton, Félix (1865–1925) Born in Lausanne and settling in Paris, he was converted from his early realist style of painting by the Japanese exhibition of 1900 and started producing highly simplified prints and engravings, many of them published in the pages of *La Revue Blanche*, and which had a profound influence on his paintings. He joined the Nabis and exhibited at Le Barc de Boutteville's and the Indépendants. He was also an anarchist.

Valtat, Louis (1869–1952) Originally influenced by Monet, he picked up, as did many of his contemporaries, influences from Gauguin and the Nabis. Working mostly in the south around St Tropez with Signac, he painted mainly brightly coloured landscapes.

Van de Velde, Henry (1863–1957) After starting his artistic training in Antwerp he worked in Paris under Carolus-Duran but came into contact with more advanced art forms, exhibiting with Les Vingt in Brussels. He then turned with great success to design and architecture and in 1907 founded the famous Weimar School of Arts and Crafts.

Verkade, Jan (1868–1946) Dutch by birth, he became associated with the Nabis and, partly through the influence of Sérusier, was converted to Catholicism. At the same time he was deeply interested in theories of harmony and proportions. In 1894 he became a Benedictine monk at the abbey of Beuron in Germany and was involved in the decoration of several churches and religious institutions.

Vlaminck, Maurice de (1876–1958) Inspired to take up painting as a result of seeing the van Gogh exhibition at Bernheim Jeune, Paris, in 1901, he forsook his earlier activities as a racing cyclist and a violinist. Initially he shared a studio with Derain at Chatou on the Seine and with him founded the so-called 'Dalou School', one of the precursors of Fauvism. Using an increasingly heavy impasto he pushed Fauvism into what might be called French Expressionism.

Vollard, Ambroise (1868–1939) Born on the island of Réunion, off Martinique, he studied law at Montpellier and, moving to Paris, became an apprentice at the gallery of the Union Artistique. He then opened his own gallery in the rue Lafitte with an exhibition of works by Manet. In 1895 he staged a show of Cézanne's works, which had a considerable success. He went on progressively to keep abreast of all the new movements in French painting, exhibiting the Nabis, van Gogh, Gauguin, Matisse, Picasso and the Cubists. He also published important books of prints.

Vuillard, Edouard (1868–1940) Studying art first at the École des Beaux-Arts and then at the Académie Julian, in 1889 he joined the Nabis, though he was not an entirely consistent follower of their ideals. He briefly fell under the influence of Gauguin and Japanese art strongly affected his work. He was particularly enamoured of painting domestic scenes in delicately modulated colours, often using sophisticated mixed techniques involving oil, pastel, temper and gouache. Owing something to Puvis de Chavannes, he undertook a certain amount of mural painting and was an active and brilliant print-maker.

Select Bibliography

ADRIANI, G., *Toulouse-Lautrec: The Complete Graphic Works*, London, 1988

ANDERSEN, W., *Gauguin's Paradise Lost*, London, 1971

BARNICOAT, J., *Posters: A Concise History*, London and New York, 1984

BARR, A. H., *Matisse: His Art and His Public*, New York, 1951

BERNARD, É., *Souvenirs*, Paris, 1939

BLANCHE, J.-E., *Les Arts plastiques, 1870 à nos jours*, Paris, 1931

Bonnard and his Environment (ed. J. Elliott), New York, 1964

CASSOU, J., E. LANGUIE and N. PEVSNER, *Sources of Modern Art*, London, 1962

Cézanne: The Late Work (ed. W. Rubin), exh. cat., Museum of Modern Art, New York, 1977

CHASSÉ, C., *Les Nabis et leur temps*, Paris, 1960

CHENNEVAL, G., *Les Nabis*, Paris, 1964

COGEVAL, G., *The Post-Impressionists*, London, 1988

COMPIN, E., *H. E. Cross*, Paris, 1964

The Complete Letters of Van Gogh, 3 vols, London and New York, 1958

Conversations avec Cézanne (ed. P. M. Doran), Paris, 1978

Correspondance de Paul Gauguin, 1873–1888 (ed. V. Merlhès), Paris, 1984

Correspondance de Camille Pissarro (ed. J. Bailly-Herzberg), Paris, 1986

DANIELSSON, B., *Gauguin in the South Seas*, London, 1965

DAUBERVILLE, D. L. and H., *Pierre Bonnard: catalogue raisonné de l'oeuvre peint*, 3 vols and supplement, Paris, 1965–75

DENIS, M., 'Définition du néo-traditionnalisme', *Art et critique*, 23 and 30 August 1890

——, *Journal, 1884–1943*, 3 vols, Paris, 1957–9

——, *Théories, 1890–1910*, Paris, 1912 (new edn 1964)

DENVIR, B., *Toulouse-Lautrec*, London and New York, 1991

DORIVAL, B., *Les Étapes de la peinture française contemporaine*, 3 vols, Paris, 1943, vol. 1, *De l'impressionnisme au fauvisme 1883–1905*

DUNLOP, I., *The Shock of the New: Seven Historic Exhibitions of Modern Art*, London, 1972

DUVAL, J.-L., *Journal de l'art moderne 1884–1914*, Geneva, 1973

ELDERFIELD, J., *The "Wild Beasts:" Fauvism and its Affinities*, New York, 1976

FÉNÉON, F. *Oeuvres plus que complètes* (ed. J. Halperin), 2 vols, Geneva and Paris, 1970

French Symbolist Painters, exh. cat., Hayward Gallery, London, 1972

Gauguin, exh. cat., National Gallery of Art, Washington D.C.; Art Institute of Chicago; Grand Palais, Paris, 1988

P. Gauguin: Lettres à sa femme et ses amis (ed. M. Malingue), Paris, 1945 (Eng. trans. H. Stennings, London [1948])

Gauguin and the School of Pont-Aven, exh. cat., Royal Academy, London, 1989

GAUZI, F., *My Friend Toulouse-Lautrec*, London, 1957

GOSLING, N., *Paris 1900–1914*, London, 1978

GOWING, L., *Matisse*, London and New York, 1979

GRUNFELD, F., *Rodin*, Oxford, 1989

HALPERIN, J., *Félix Fénéon: Aesthete and Anarchist in Fin de Siècle Paris*, New Haven, CT, 1989

HARTRICK, A. S., *A Painter's Pilgrimage through Fifty Years*, Cambridge, 1938

HERBERT, E. W., *The Artist and Social Reform: France and Belgium, 1865–1898*, New Haven, CT, 1961

HOBBS, R., *Odilon Redon*, London, 1977

HOFFMANN, W., *The Earthly Paradise: Art in the Nineteenth Century*, London, 1961

HUYSMANS, J.-K., *Certains*, Paris, 1889

——, *L'Art moderne*, Paris 1883

IVES, C. F., *The Great Wave: the Influence of Japanese Woodcuts on French Prints*, Metropolitan Museum of Art, New York, 1974

JACOBS, M., *The Good and Simple Life: Artists' Colonies*, Oxford, 1985

Japonisme in Art: An International Symposium (ed. Y. Chisaburo), Tokyo, 1980

JAWORSKA, W., *Gauguin and the Pont-Aven School*, Boston, 1972

LASSAIGNE, J., *Toulouse-Lautrec and the Paris of Cabarets*, New York, 1970

LEHMANN, A. G., *The Symbolist Aesthetic in France, 1885–1895*, Oxford, 1968

The Letters of Cézanne (ed. J. Rewald), New York, 1984

The Letters of Paul Gauguin to Daniel de Monfreid (trans. R. Pielkovo), New York, 1922

Lettres de Paul Gauguin à Émile Bernard 1888–91, Geneva, 1954

Lettres d'Odilon Redon, Brussels and Paris, 1923

LÖVGREN, S., *The Genesis of Modernism: Seurat, Gauguin, Van Gogh and French Symbolism in the 1880s*, Uppsala, 1959

LUCIE-SMITH, E., *Symbolist Art*, London and New York, 1972

Henri Matisse. Écrits et propos sur l'art (ed. D. Fourcade), Paris, 1972

MATTHIEU, P.-L., *Gustave Moreau*, Oxford, 1977

MAUNER, G., *The Nabis, their History and their Art, 1888–1896*, London and New York, 1978

MAUS, M. O., *Trente Années de lutte pour l'art, 1884–1914*, Brussels, 1926

MORICE, C., *Gauguin*, Paris, 1920

NATANSON, T., *Peints à leur tour*, Paris, 1948

Neo-Impressionism, exh. cat. by R. Herbert, Solomon R. Guggenheim Museum, New York, 1968

PERRUCHOT, H., *La Vie de Gauguin*, Paris, 1961

PINCUS-WITTEN, R., *Occult Symbolism in France: Joséphin Péladan and the Salons de la Rose + Croix*, New York and London, 1976

Post-Impressionism, exh. cat., Royal Academy, London, 1979–80

PRAZ, M., *The Romantic Agony*, London, 2nd edn 1951

REDON, O., *À soi-même*, Paris, repr. 1961

REWALD, J., *Paul Cézanne*, London and New York, 1986

——, *The History of Impressionism*, London and New York, 1961

——, *Post-Impressionism: From Van Gogh to Gauguin*, New York and London, 1956

——, *Seurat*, New York and London, 1990

ROOKMAAKER, H. R., *Gauguin and Nineteenth Century French Art Theory*, Amsterdam, 1959 (2nd edn 1972)

ROSENBLUM, R., *Modern Painting and the Northern Romantic Tradition*, London and New York, 1975

ROSKILL, M., *Van Gogh, Gauguin and the Impressionist Circle*, London, 1970

ROTHENSTEIN, W., *Men and Memories*, 2 vols, London, 1931–2 (rev. edn, ed. M. Lago, 1978)

RUBIN, W., *Primitivism in 20th Century Art*, New York, 1984

RUSSELL, J., *Vuillard, 1868–1940*, London, 1971

SAID, E., *Orientalism*, New York, 1978

SEITZ, W. C., *Claude Monet: Seasons and Moments*, New York, 1960

Seurat, exh. cat., Grand Palais, Paris, 1991

SHATTUCK, R., *The Banquet Years*, London, 1959

SHIFF, R., *Cézanne and the End of Impressionism*, Chicago, 1984

SIGNAC, P., *D'Eugène Delacroix au néo-impressionnisme*, Paris, 1899 (new edn, ed. F. Cachin, 1964)

SMITH, B., *European Vision and the South Pacific*, New Haven, CT, and London, 2nd edn 1985

SUTTER, J., *The Neo-Impressionists*, London, 1970

THOMSON, B., *Gauguin*, London and New York, 1987

——, *The Post-Impressionists*, Oxford, 1983

——, *Vuillard*, Oxford, 1988

Vincent van Gogh: paintings and drawings, 2 vols, exh. cat., Rijksmuseum Vincent van Gogh, Amsterdam, 1990

VOLLARD, A., *Souvenirs d'un marchand des tableaux*, Paris, 1937

WHITFIELD, S., *Fauvism*, London and New York, 1991

WICHMANN, S., *Japonisme: The Japanese Influence on Western Art since 1858*, London, 1981

WITTROCK, W., *Toulouse-Lautrec: The Complete Prints*, London, 1985

World Cultures and Modern Art: The Encounter of 19th and 20th Century European Art and Music with Asia, Africa, Oceania, Afro- and Indo-America, exh. cat., Haus der Kunst, Munich, 1972

ZELDIN, T., *France 1848–1945*, 2 vols, Oxford, 1979–80

List of Illustrations

Measurements are in centimetres and inches, height before depth, unless otherwise stated

1 'Post-Impressionist Expressions', *Illustrated London News* 3 December 1910

2 Roger Fry *A Room at the 2nd Post-Impressionist Exhibition* 1912. Oil on wood, 50.8 × 61 (20 × 24). Musée d'Orsay, Paris. Photo Réunion des musées nationaux

3 Georges Seurat *Model seated in Profile* 1887. Oil on panel, 25 × 17.4 ($9\frac{7}{8}$ × $6\frac{5}{8}$). Musée d'Orsay, Paris. Photo Giraudon

4 Federigo Zandomeneghi *Place d'Anvers, Paris* 1880. Oil on canvas, 102 × 136 ($40\frac{1}{8}$ × $53\frac{1}{2}$). Galleria d'Arte Moderna Ricci-Oddi, Piacenza

5 Georges Seurat *Une Baignade à Asnières* 1883–4. Oil on canvas, 2 × 2.9 m ($6\frac{1}{2}$ × $9\frac{3}{4}$ ft). National Gallery, London

6 Paul Signac *The Dining-room: Breakfast* 1886–7. Oil on canvas, 89 × 115 (35 × $45\frac{1}{4}$). State Museum, Kröller-Müller, Otterlo, The Netherlands

7 Signac *Les femmes au puit* 1892. Oil on canvas, 194 × 130 ($76\frac{3}{8}$ × $51\frac{1}{4}$). Musée d'Orsay, Paris. Photo Réunion des musées nationaux

8 Armand Guillaumin *Le Pont de Marie* 1883. Oil on canvas, 49 × 67 ($19\frac{1}{4}$ × $26\frac{3}{8}$). Musée du Petit Palais, Geneva

9 Camille Pissarro *Femme dans un clos, soleil de printemps dans le pré* 1887. Oil on canvas, 54 × 65 ($21\frac{1}{4}$ × $25\frac{1}{2}$). Musée d'Orsay, Paris. Photo Réunion des musées nationaux

10 Henri-Edmond Cross *The Excursionists* 1894. Oil on canvas, 65 × 92 ($25\frac{1}{2}$ × $36\frac{1}{4}$). Musée du Petit Palais, Geneva

11 Georges Seurat *La Grande Jatte* 1883–6. Oil on canvas, 2.1 × 3.1 m ($6\frac{3}{4}$ × $10\frac{1}{8}$ ft). The Art Institute of Chicago, Helen Birch Bartlett Memorial Collection

12 Edgar Degas *Woman drying Herself* 1885. Pastel, 80.1 × 51.2 ($31\frac{1}{2}$ × $20\frac{1}{8}$). National Gallery of Art, Washington D.C., Gift of the W. Averell Harriman Foundation

13 Georges Seurat *The Bathers, c.* 1883, study for *Une Baignade.* Oil on panel, 15.9 × 25 ($6\frac{1}{4}$ × $9\frac{7}{8}$). Collection Mr and Mrs Paul Mellon, Upperville, VA

14 Henri-Edmond Cross *L'Air du Soir* 1893–4. Oil on canvas, 116 × 164 ($45\frac{5}{8}$ × $64\frac{1}{2}$). Musée d'Orsay, Paris. Photo Réunion des musées nationaux

15 Paul Cézanne *Still Life with Onions and a Bottle* 1895–1900. Oil on canvas, 66 × 82 (30 × $32\frac{1}{4}$). Musée d'Orsay, Paris. Photo Réunion des musées nationaux

16 Maurice Denis *Homage to Cézanne* 1900. Oil on canvas, 180 × 240 (71 × 95). Musée d'Orsay, Paris. Photo Réunion des musées nationaux

17 Paul Cézanne *The Large Bather, c.* 1885. Oil on canvas, 127 × 96.8 (50 × $38\frac{1}{8}$). The Museum of Modern Art, New York, Lillie P. Bliss Collection

18 Vincent van Gogh *The Night Café* 1888. Oil on canvas, 70 × 89 ($27\frac{1}{2}$ × 35). Yale University Art Gallery, Bequest of Stephen Carlton Clark

19 Paul Gauguin *Night Café at Arles* 1888. Oil on canvas, 73 × 92 ($28\frac{3}{4}$ × $36\frac{1}{4}$). Pushkin Museum, Moscow

20 Vincent van Gogh *L'Arlésienne* 1888. Oil on canvas, 90 × 72 ($35\frac{1}{2}$ × $28\frac{1}{4}$). Metropolitan Museum of Art, New York, Bequest of Sam A. Lewisohn

21 Pierre Puvis de Chavannes *The Sacred Grove* 1884. Oil on canvas, 5.8 × 10.2 m (19 × $33\frac{1}{3}$ ft). Musée des Beaux-Arts, Lyons

22 Pierre Bonnard *France-Champagne* 1889, poster. Lithograph, 76.5 × 58.4 ($30\frac{1}{8}$ × 23)

23 Henri de Toulouse-Lautrec *At the Cirque Fernando: Rider* 1888. Oil on canvas, 98.4 × 161.3 ($38\frac{3}{4}$ × $63\frac{1}{2}$). The Art Institute of Chicago, Joseph Winterbotham Collection

24 Georges Seurat *The Circus* 1890–91. Oil on canvas, 186 × 151 ($73\frac{1}{4}$ × $59\frac{1}{2}$). Musée d'Orsay, Paris. Photo Bulloz

25 Théo van Rysselberghe *Portrait of Octave Maus* 1885. Oil on canvas, 90.5 × 75.5 ($35\frac{5}{8}$ × $29\frac{3}{4}$). Musées Royaux des Beaux-Arts, Brussels

26 Fernand Khnopff *Les XX* 1891, poster

27 Henri de Toulouse-Lautrec *Mlle Marcelle Lender* 1895, poster. Colour lithograph

28 Toulouse-Lautrec *Aristide Bruant dans son cabaret* 1892, poster. Colour lithograph

29 Alphonse Mucha *Salon des Cent* 1896, poster

30 Georges Seurat *Lighthouse at Honfleur* 1886. Oil on canvas, 66.7 × 81.9 ($26\frac{1}{4}$ × $32\frac{1}{4}$). National Gallery of Art, Washington D.C., Collection Mr and Mrs Paul Mellon

31 Henri Rousseau ('le Douanier') *La Charmeuse de serpents* 1907. Oil on canvas, 169 × 189.5 ($66\frac{5}{8} \times 74\frac{3}{4}$). Musée d'Orsay, Paris. Photo Giraudon

32 *L'Illustration* 4 November 1905, on the Salon d'Automne. Mansell Collection

33 Paul Cézanne *Bathers Resting* 1876–7. Oil on canvas, 79 × 97.1 ($31\frac{1}{8} \times 38\frac{1}{4}$). Barnes Foundation, Merion, Pennsylvania

34 Henri Rousseau ('le Douanier') *The Hungry Lion . . .* 1905. Oil on canvas, 201.5 × 301.5 ($79\frac{3}{8} \times 118\frac{3}{4}$). Öffentliche Kunstsammlung, Basel Kunstmuseum

35 *Medieval Ball at l'Elysée Montmartre*, from *Le Courrier Français* 1893. Bibliothèque Nationale, Paris

36 The first woman bill-poster in Paris

37 Maximilien Luce *View of Montmartre* 1887. Oil on canvas, 45.4 × 81 (18 × 32). State Museum, Kröller-Müller, Otterlo, The Netherlands

38 Lucien Pissarro *Soup* (the Café Nouvelles-Athènes or the Café Volpini) 1889. Crayon, 14.8 × 20.3 ($5\frac{3}{4} \times 8$). Courtesy Anthony d'Offay Gallery, London

39 Georges Seurat *Eden Concert* 1887–8. Conté crayon, 29.7 × 22.9 ($11\frac{3}{4} \times 9$). Vincent van Gogh Foundation/Vincent van Gogh Museum, Amsterdam

40 Pierre Bonnard *The Cab-horse*, *c.* 1895. Oil on wood, 29.7 × 40 ($11\frac{3}{4} \times 15\frac{3}{4}$). National Gallery of Art, Washington D.C., Ailsa Mellon Bruce Collection 1970

41 Paul Gauguin *Aux Roches noires*, frontispiece of the Volpini exhibition catalogue, 1889

42 Louis Anquetin *Avenue de Clichy, 5 O'clock in the Evening* 1887. Oil on canvas, 69 × 53 (27 × 21). Courtesy Wadsworth Atheneum, Hartford, CT, Ella Gallup Sumner and Mary Catlin Sumner Collection

43 Marcellin Desboutin *Sâr Péladan* 1891. Oil on canvas. Musée des Beaux-Arts, Angers

44 Carlos Schwabe *Salon de la Rose + Croix* 1892, poster

45 Paul Cézanne *Portrait of A. Vollard* 1899. Oil on canvas, 99 × 78.7 (39 × 31). Musée du Petit Palais, Paris. Photo Bulloz

46 Émile Bernard *Portrait of Père Tanguy* 1887. Oil on canvas, 36 × 31 ($14\frac{1}{4} \times 12\frac{1}{4}$). Öffentliche Kunstsammlung, Basel Kunstmuseum

47 Maurice Denis *La Dépêche de Toulouse* 1892?, poster. 154 × 97 ($60\frac{5}{8} \times 38\frac{1}{8}$)

48 Odilon Redon *Portrait of Paul Sérusier* 1903. Drawing

49 Redon *Portrait of Maurice Denis* 1903. Lithograph, 15.3 × 13.5 ($6\frac{1}{8} \times 5\frac{5}{8}$). The Art Institute of Chicago, E. H. Stickney Fund

50 Redon *Portrait of Pierre Bonnard* 1902. Lithograph, 14.5 × 12.3 ($5\frac{3}{4} \times 4\frac{5}{8}$). The Art Institute of Chicago, E. H. Stickney Fund

51 Paul Gauguin *Idole à la perle* 1892–3. Tamunu wood, stained and gilded, 25 ($9\frac{7}{8}$) h. Musée d'Orsay, Paris. Photo Réunion des musées nationaux

52 Katsushika Hokusai, 'The Goddess Konohana Sakuya Hime', no. 1 from *One Hundred Views of Mount Fuji* 1830s

53 Vincent van Gogh *Japonaiserie: Oiran* 1887. Oil on wood, 105 × 61 ($41\frac{1}{2} \times 24$). Vincent van Gogh Foundation/Vincent van Gogh Museum, Amsterdam

54 Le Japon, cover of *Paris Illustré* May 1866. Vincent van Gogh Foundation/Vincent van Gogh Museum, Amsterdam

55 Vincent van Gogh *La Segatori au Café Tambourin* 1887. Oil on canvas, 55.4 × 46.5 ($21\frac{3}{4} \times 18\frac{1}{4}$). Vincent van Gogh Foundation/Vincent van Gogh Museum, Amsterdam

56 Mary Cassatt *In the Omnibus* 1891. Colour print with drypoint, soft ground and aquatint, 36 × 27 ($14\frac{1}{4} \times 10\frac{1}{2}$). The Art Institute of Chicago, Martin A. Ryerson Collection

57 Louis Anquetin *Girl reading a Newspaper* 1890. Pastel on paper on millboard, 54 × 43.5 ($21\frac{1}{4} \times 17\frac{1}{8}$). Tate Gallery, London

58 Henri de Toulouse-Lautrec in Japanese samurai costume, *c.* 1892. Bibliothèque Nationale, Paris. Photo M. Guibert

59 Danjuro VII *Actor in a Shibaraku Role, c.* 1820. Colour woodcut with mica and brass powder, surinomo, 20.3 × 17.8 (8 × 7). Metropolitan Museum of Art, New York, Rogers Fund, 1922

60 Henri de Toulouse-Lautrec *Miss Loïe Fuller* 1893, poster. Colour lithograph

61 Pierre Bonnard *Street Corner*, from *Quelques aspects de la vie de Paris* 1899. Colour lithograph. Metropolitan Museum

of Art, New York, Harris Brisbane Dick Fund, 1928

62 Edouard Vuillard *The Avenue*, from *Paysages et intérieurs* 1899. Colour lithograph, 31 × 41.2 ($12\frac{1}{4} \times 16\frac{1}{4}$). Courtesy Agnew's

63 Vuillard *The Seamstress*, c. 1893. Colour lithograph, wood-engraving and woodcut. Metropolitan Museum of Art, New York, Elisha Whittelsey Fund, 1973

64 Suzuki Harunobu *Youth playing a Drum* 1768. Woodblock print, 44.1 × 20.6 ($17\frac{3}{8} \times 8\frac{1}{8}$). Metropolitan Museum of Art, New York, The H. O. Havemeyer Collection, Bequest of Mrs H. O. Havemeyer, 1929

65 Paul Gauguin *The Vision after the Sermon: The Struggle of Jacob and the Angel* 1888. Oil on canvas, 73 × 92 ($28\frac{3}{4} \times 36\frac{1}{4}$). National Galleries of Scotland, Edinburgh

66 Vincent van Gogh *Italian Woman* 1887–8. Oil on canvas, 81 × 60 ($31\frac{7}{8} \times 23\frac{5}{8}$). Musée d'Orsay, Paris. Photo Réunion des musées nationaux

67 Lucien Pissarro *Copy after Egyptian Fresco*, c. 1880. 29 × 22.6 ($73\frac{5}{8} \times 57\frac{3}{8}$). Ashmolean Museum, Oxford

68 Fang mask from Gabon, which belonged to Vlaminck and Derain. Musée National d'Art Moderne, Centre Georges Pompidou, Paris

69 Magazine photograph used by Matisse for his *Two Negresses* sculpture of 1908

70 Palais des colonies, 1889 Universal Exhibition, Paris. From E. Monod, *Livre d'Or de l'Exposition Universelle Album*, 1890

71 Auguste Rodin *Drawing of a Cambodian Dancer* 1906. From *L'Illustration*, 1906. Mansell Collection

72 Rodin drawing a Cambodian dancer, from *L'Illustration*, 1906. Mansell Collection

73 A Breton calvary, Menhir de Pleuven. Photo Musée de Bretagne, Rennes

74 Paul Gauguin *Self-Portrait with Yellow Christ* 1889. Oil on canvas, 38 × 46 ($15 \times 18\frac{1}{8}$). Private collection. Photo Giraudon

75 Gauguin *Luxury* 1890. Oak with gilding, 70.5 ($27\frac{3}{4}$) h. J. F. Willumsens Museum, Frederikssund

76 Gauguin *Aha Oe Feii?* (What, are you jealous?), 1892. Oil on canvas, 68 × 92 ($26\frac{3}{4} \times 36\frac{1}{4}$). Pushkin Museum, Moscow

77 Paul Cézanne *The Murderer* 1867. Oil on canvas, 65.4 × 81.2 ($25\frac{3}{4} \times 32$). The Board of Trustees of the National Museums and Galleries on Merseyside

78 Cézanne *Portrait of Achille Emperaire*, c. 1868–70. Oil on canvas, 200 × 122 ($78\frac{3}{4} \times 48$). Musée d'Orsay, Paris. Photo Galerie Bernheim-Jeune

79 Henri Rousseau ('le Douanier') *Myself: Landscape Portrait* 1890. Oil on canvas, 143 × 110 ($56\frac{1}{4} \times 43\frac{1}{4}$). National Gallery, Prague

80 Interior of the café Le Lapin Agile, Paris, early 1900s

81 Paul Ranson *Christ and Buddha* 1895. Oil on canvas, 66.7 × 51.4 ($26\frac{1}{4} \times 20\frac{1}{4}$). Collection of Mr and Mrs Arthur G. Altschul, New York

82 Hubert van Herkomer *Hard Times* 1885. Oil on canvas, 86.5 × 112 ($34 \times 44\frac{1}{8}$). City Art Gallery, Manchester

83 Jean-Louis-Ernest Meissonier *The Barricades: Rue de la Mortellerie, June 1848*. Oil on canvas, 29 × 22 ($11\frac{1}{2} \times 8\frac{1}{2}$). Musée du Louvre, Paris. Photo Giraudon

84 Alphonse Osbert *The Vision* 1892. Oil on canvas, 2.8 × 1.8 m ($9\frac{1}{4} \times 5\frac{3}{4}$ ft). Private collection

85 Gustave Moreau *Young Girl carrying the Head of Orpheus* 1865. Oil on canvas, 154 × 99.5 ($60\frac{5}{8} \times 39\frac{1}{8}$). Musée d'Orsay, Paris. Photo Bulloz

86 Moreau *Mystic Flower*, c. 1890. Oil on canvas, 2.3 × 1.4 m ($7\frac{1}{2} \times 4\frac{1}{2}$ ft). Musée Gustave Moreau, Paris. Photo Bulloz

87 Paul Sérusier *Tobias and the Angel*, c. 1895. Oil on canvas, 112 × 69 ($44 \times 27\frac{1}{4}$). James Kirkman Ltd

88 Lucien Lévy-Dhurmer *Our Lady of Penmarc'h* 1896. Oil on canvas, 41 × 33 ($16\frac{1}{4} \times 13$). Private collection

89 Maurice Denis *Catholic Mystery* 1890. Oil on canvas, 57 × 77 ($20 \times 30\frac{1}{4}$). J. F. Denis collection, Alençon

90 Charles Filiger *Virgin and Child*, c. 1892. Gouache on panel, 31 × 25 ($12\frac{1}{4} \times 9\frac{7}{8}$). Collection Mr and Mrs Arthur G. Altschul, New York

91 Émile Bernard *Bretonneries*, zincograph cover of album, 1889. 33 × 25 ($13 \times 9\frac{7}{8}$). Musée des Beaux-Arts, Quimper

92 Pierre Puvis de Chavannes *The Dream* 1883. Oil on canvas, 82 × 102 ($32\frac{1}{4} \times 40\frac{1}{8}$). Musée d'Orsay, Paris. Photo Réunion des musées nationaux

93 Paul Sérusier *Portrait of Jan Verkade* 1906. Oil on canvas, 102×75 ($40\frac{1}{4} \times 29\frac{1}{2}$). Musée d'Orsay, Paris

94 Paul Gauguin *Hail Mary*, woodcut in *Noa Noa* 1893. Musée du Louvre, Cabinet des Dessins, Paris. Photo Réunion des musées nationaux

95 Camille Pissarro, drawing for cover of *Turpitudes Sociales* 1890. Pen and ink, 31.5×24.5 ($12\frac{3}{8} \times 9\frac{5}{8}$). Private collection

96 Félix Vallotton *The Riot* 1893. Woodcut, 20.3×31.7 ($8 \times 12\frac{1}{2}$). Bibliothèque Nationale, Paris

97 Vallotton *Fénéon in the office of La Revue Blanche* 1896. Oil on cardboard, 52.5×65 ($20\frac{5}{8} \times 25\frac{1}{2}$). Josefowitz Collection

98 Angelo Morbelli *For 80 Cents* 1895. Oil on canvas, 70×124 ($27\frac{1}{2} \times 48\frac{3}{4}$). Civico Museo Antonio Borgogna, Vercelli

99 Fernand Cormon *The Forge* 1893. Oil on canvas, 59×78 ($23\frac{1}{4} \times 30\frac{3}{4}$). Musée d'Orsay, Paris. Photo Réunion des musées nationaux

100 Maximilien Luce *Workman washing Himself* 1886–7. Oil on canvas, 92×73 ($36\frac{1}{4} \times 28\frac{3}{4}$). Musée du Petit Palais, Geneva

101 Théophile-Alexandre Steinlen *La Feuille*, *c.* 1898, poster. 144×194 ($56\frac{5}{8} \times 76\frac{3}{8}$)

102 Henri de Toulouse-Lautrec *Le Dernier Salut*, cover for *Le Mirliton*, March 1887

103 Gustave Moreau *The Apparition* 1874–6. Oil on canvas, 142×103 ($56 \times 40\frac{1}{2}$). Musée Gustave Moreau. Photo Bulloz

104 Edouard Vuillard *At the Revue Blanche* 1901. Oil on board, 46.3×57.5 ($18\frac{1}{4} \times 23$). Solomon R. Guggenheim Museum, New York, Hilla Rebay Collection. Photo David Heald

105 Pierre Bonnard, cover of *La Revue Blanche* 1894. Colour lithograph, 77.3×58.9 ($30\frac{1}{2} \times 23\frac{1}{4}$). Bibliothèque Nationale, Paris

106 Henri-Edmond Cross *Nocturne* 1896. Oil on canvas, 92×65 ($36\frac{1}{4} \times 25\frac{1}{2}$). Musée du Petit Palais, Geneva

107 Ker-Xavier Roussel *Composition: Women in the Forest* 1890–92. Oil on canvas, 44×31 ($17\frac{3}{8} \times 12\frac{1}{4}$). Musée départmental du Prieuré, St Germain-en-Laye. Photo Réunion des musées nationaux

108 Paul Gauguin *Portrait of Stéphane Mallarmé* 1891. Etching on copper, 18.2×14.3 ($7\frac{1}{8} \times 5\frac{5}{8}$). The Art Institute of Chicago, Albert H. Wolf Memorial Collection

109 Odilon Redon, 1889 illustration for Flaubert's *La Tentation de Saint Antoine*. Lithograph, 30.3×21.1 ($12 \times 8\frac{1}{4}$). Bibliothèque Nationale, Paris

110 Redon, 'Perhaps nature first tried eyes on flowers', no. 2 from *Les Origines* 1883. Lithograph

111 Redon *Evocation of Roussel*, *c.* 1912. Oil on canvas, 73.4×54.3 ($28\frac{7}{8} \times 21\frac{3}{8}$). National Gallery of Art, Washington D.C., Chester Dale Collection

112 Giovanni Segantini *Punishment of the Lustful* 1891. Oil on canvas, 99×172.8 (39×68). The Board of Trustees of the National Museums and Galleries on Merseyside

113 Maurice Denis, 1891 illustration for Verlaine's *Sagesse*. Wood-engraving. Bibliothèque Nationale, Paris

114 Paul Signac *Against the Enamel of a Background Rhythmic with Beats and Angles, Tones and Colours, Portrait of Félix Fénéon in 1890*. 73.9×93.1 ($29\frac{1}{8} \times 36\frac{5}{8}$). Private collection

115 Félicien Rops *Pornocrates* 1896. Etching and aquatint, 45×69 ($17\frac{3}{4} \times 27\frac{1}{8}$)

116 Félix Vallotton *Portrait of Thadée Natanson* 1897. Oil on canvas, 66.5×46 ($26\frac{1}{8} \times 18\frac{1}{8}$). Musée du Petit Palais, Geneva

117 Henri de Toulouse-Lautrec *La Revue Blanche* 1895, poster (Misia Natanson). Colour lithograph

118 Fernand Khnopff *The Offering* 1891. Pastel, 32×72 ($12\frac{1}{2} \times 28\frac{1}{2}$). Private collection

119 Henri Rousseau ('le Douanier') *Eve*, *c.* 1905–07. Oil on canvas, 61×46 (24×18). Kunsthalle, Hamburg

120 Edouard Vuillard, programme for the Théâtre Libre, Paris, 1890. Lithograph, 19×16.5 ($7\frac{1}{2} \times 6\frac{1}{2}$). Private collection

121 Félix Vallotton *Ibsen* 1894. Woodcut, 16×12.5 ($6\frac{1}{2} \times 5$)

122 Jean Delville *Parsifal* 1890. Charcoal, 69.8×55.9 ($27\frac{1}{2} \times 22$). Private collection. Photo courtesy Piccadilly Gallery, London

123 Paul Cézanne *Overture to Tannhäuser*, *c.* 1869–70. Oil on canvas, 57×92 ($22\frac{1}{2} \times 36\frac{1}{4}$). Hermitage State Museum, Leningrad

124 Paul Sérusier *Melancholia*, *c.* 1890. Oil on canvas, 71×57 ($28 \times 22\frac{1}{2}$). Musée d'Orsay, Paris. Photo Réunion des musées nationaux

125 Odilon Redon *The Sleep of Caliban*. Oil on wood, 44.5 × 39 ($17\frac{1}{2} \times 15\frac{3}{8}$). Musée d'Orsay, Paris. Photo Réunion des musées nationaux

126 Paul Gauguin *Loss of Virginity* 1890. Oil on canvas, 90 × 130 ($35\frac{1}{2} \times 51\frac{1}{4}$). Chrysler Museum, Norfolk, VA, Gift of Walter P. Chrysler, Jr

127 Vincent van Gogh *Lieutenant Milliet* 1888. Oil on canvas, 60 × 49 ($23\frac{1}{2} \times 19\frac{1}{4}$). State Museum, Kröller-Müller, Otterlo, The Netherlands

128 Albert Marquet *Sergeant of the Colonial Army* 1907. Oil on canvas, 90.2 × 71.1 ($35\frac{1}{2} \times 28$). Metropolitan Museum of Art, New York, Robert Lehman Collection, 1975

129 Charles Laval *Self-Portrait with Landscape: à l'ami Vincent* 1888. Oil on canvas, 50.1 × 60.1 ($19\frac{3}{4} \times 23\frac{5}{8}$). Vincent van Gogh Foundation/Vincent van Gogh Museum, Amsterdam

130 Paul Sérusier *The Talisman (Landscape in the Bois d' Amour)* 1888. Oil on panel, 27 × 22 ($10\frac{5}{8} \times 8\frac{5}{8}$). Musée d'Orsay, Paris. Photo Réunion des musées nationaux

131 Jacob Meyer de Haan *Farm at Le Pouldu* 1889. Oil on canvas, 73.5 × 93 ($29 \times 36\frac{5}{8}$). State Museum, Kröller-Müller, Otterlo, The Netherlands

132 Charles Filiger *Landscape at Le Pouldu* 1895. Gouache on paper, 26 × 38.5 ($10\frac{1}{4} \times 15\frac{1}{8}$). Musée des Beaux-Arts, Quimper

133 Émile Bernard *The Buckwheat Harvest* 1888. Oil on canvas, 73 × 90 ($28\frac{3}{4} \times 35\frac{1}{2}$). Josefowitz Collection

134 Eugène Carrière *Motherhood*, *c.* 1890. Oil on canvas, 38.1 × 30.4 (15×12). National Museum of Wales, Cardiff

135 Félix Vallotton *The Balloon* 1899. Oil on canvas, 48 × 60 ($18\frac{7}{8} \times 23\frac{5}{8}$). Musée d'Orsay, Paris. Photo Réunion des musées nationaux

136 Henri Matisse *Luxe, calme et volupté* 1904. Oil on canvas, 98 × 118 ($38\frac{5}{8} \times 46\frac{1}{2}$). Musée d'Orsay, Paris. Photo Réunion des musées nationaux

137 Henry van de Velde *Woman at a Window* 1890. Oil on canvas, 111 × 125 ($43\frac{3}{4} \times 49\frac{1}{4}$). Koninklijk Museum voor Schone Kunsten, Antwerp

138 Edvard Munch *The Dance of Life* 1899. Oil on canvas, 125.5 × 190.5 ($49\frac{3}{8} \times 75$). Nasjonalgalleriet, Oslo

139 Odilon Redon *Portrait of Gauguin* 1904. Oil on canvas, 66 × 44 ($26 \times 17\frac{3}{8}$). Musée d'Orsay, Paris. Photo Réunion des musées nationaux

140 André Derain *Effects of Sun on Water* 1905. Oil on canvas, 78.1 × 100 ($30\frac{3}{4} \times 39\frac{3}{8}$). Musée de l'Annonciade, St Tropez. Photo Réunion des musées nationaux

141 Maurice de Vlaminck *La Seine à Chatou* 1905. Oil on canvas, 64 × 80 ($25\frac{1}{8} \times 31\frac{1}{2}$). Private collection. Photo courtesy Robert Schmit, Paris

142 Raoul Dufy *Jeanne with Flowers*, *c.* 1907. Oil on canvas, 90 × 78 ($35\frac{3}{8} \times 30\frac{3}{4}$). Musée des Beaux-Arts, Le Havre

143 Georges Braque *Landscape at L'Estaque* 1907. Oil on canvas, 37 × 46 ($14\frac{1}{2} \times 18\frac{1}{8}$). Musée d'Art Moderne de Troyes

144 Emile-Othon Friesz *Landscape at La Ciotat* 1907. Oil on canvas, 65 × 81 ($25\frac{1}{2} \times 31\frac{7}{8}$). Musée d'Art Moderne de Troyes

145 André Derain *Portrait of Vlaminck* 1905. Oil on canvas, 27.3 × 22.2 ($10\frac{3}{4} \times 8\frac{3}{4}$). Private collection

146 Henri Matisse *Les Toits de Collioure* 1906. Oil on canvas, 59.3 × 73 ($23\frac{3}{8} \times 28\frac{3}{4}$). Hermitage State Museum, Leningrad

147 Claude Monet *Haystacks* 1890–91. Oil on canvas, 65.1 × 92.1 ($25\frac{5}{8} \times 36\frac{1}{4}$). Private collection

148 Wassily Kandinsky *Blue Mountain* 1908. Oil on canvas, 106 × 96.6 ($41\frac{3}{4} \times 38$). Solomon R. Guggenheim Museum, New York, Gift of Solomon R. Guggenheim, 1941. Photo Robert E. Mates

Works by the following artists © 1992 SPADEM: Maurice Denis, Raoul Dufy, Ker-Xavier Roussel
Works by the following artists © 1992 ADAGP: Pierre Bonnard, Georges Braque, Emile-Othon Friesz, Wassily Kandinsky, Albert Marquet, Maurice de Vlaminck
Works by Matisse © 1992 Succession Henri Matisse

Index

Italic numerals refer to plate numbers